✳ Jean Cocteau
and the French Scene

*Jean

Cocteau
and the French Scene

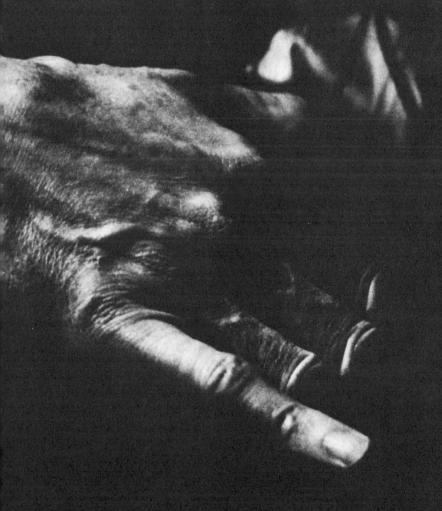

Abbeville Press • Publishers • New York

Project editors: Alexandra Anderson, Carol Saltus
Art director: Howard Morris
Designer: Victoria Arthur
Picture researcher: Christopher Sweet
Production manager: Dana Cole
Production editor: Robin James

JACKET FRONT: George Platt Lynes. Jean Cocteau, c. 1930
JACKET BACK: Cocteau's house at Milly-la-Forêt, 1953
TITLE PAGE: The hands of Jean Cocteau

Library of Congress Cataloging in Publication Data

Main entry under title:

Jean Cocteau and the French scene.

Includes index.
1. Cocteau, Jean, 1889–1963. 2. Authors, French—20th
century—Biography. 3. France—Intellectual life—20th
century. I. Ashton, Doré.
PQ2605.015Z6863   1984   848'.91209 [B] 83-73421
ISBN 0-89659-412-2

First edition
Printed and bound in the U.S.A.

Contents

✳ Jean Cocteau
and the French Scene

Paul Strand. *Jean Cocteau, Saint-Jean-Cap-Ferrat, Alpes-Maritime, France,* 1956
Collection Walter and Naomi Rosenblum

Preface

Arthur King Peters

I NEVER SET EYES ON JEAN COCTEAU. That was probably just as well, because then I could see him more objectively. His slim, elegant figure and brilliant conversational fireworks couldn't dazzle me as they had others. The aristocratic face beneath the electrified hair that frizzed out of control in all directions, the large, intelligent, hazel eyes, curiously ringed with a thin, milky line around the iris, were known to me only from photographs. So were the long-boned Gothic hands projecting from always turned-up cuffs—the hands of a surgeon, a violinist, a croupier, or a magician. If not in fact, Jean Cocteau in spirit was all these things, and more. He was also homosexual, and a smoker of opium. He was nine when his father shot himself to death.

Who is to separate cause from effect?

Though I never met Jean Cocteau, I came to know him well. I wanted to learn what set him apart from every other artist.

What made him tick. Where he lived. I dogged his footsteps from London, where he drew murals for the beautiful little church of Notre-Dame-de-France just off Trafalgar Square, to the Hotel Minerva in Rome, where he and Picasso worked in 1917 on the bombshell ballet *Parade* for the Ballets Russes. It was there that Picasso courted his first wife Olga; Cocteau placed a coronet on her head at the wedding ceremony. My trail led from Paris to the Riviera, from the Hotel de Castille on the rue Cambon (where he could be near his friend Coco Chanel) to the Hotel Welcome in Villefranche. There the American Sixth Fleet anchored in 1926 for shore leave. Pandemonium ensued. Cocteau describes the bedlam of the fleet's departure:

> I'm living in a weird place—a box completely suspended in the upper branches of a blazing Christmas tree. On the first floor of the hotel-bordello, day and night the sailors brawl and do the belly dance. The only jazz I hear is the bass drum; it's as though they were printing a newspaper in the cellars. Engine din, the tarts' hysterics, the sailors' choruses . . . etc. . . . The departure of the *Pittsburgh* was a dream, with the "Marseillaise" played in slow time and twelve searchlights on the strumpets [sic] sobbing in the hotel windows . . .

It was at Villefranche, in the chapel of St. Peter dedicated to simple fishermen, that Cocteau first began to decorate chapels with his limpid line murals, the last being his own final resting place in St. Blaise des Simples at Milly-la-Forêt. Cocteau died before he could finish the most beautiful of all, the hexagonal chapel that rests like a stone crown on the brow of the hill above Fréjus. It is to be hoped that the French authorities will soon see to its completion.

After a much overdue escape from his mother's Paris apartment, for long stretches Cocteau led a nomadic life, moving from hotel to hotel or visiting friends when his allowance from home ran out. The story of his long and close relationship with his mother remains to be told. We know he wrote her over a thousand letters, sometimes three a day, and for many years sent as a Christmas present a new poem composed just for her. For Mme. Cocteau, a respectable bourgeois widow, Jean must have been a gifted *"enfant terrible,"* seething with problems and talents. He first became aware of his sexual ambivalence when as a child he fainted at the sight of a naked farm boy. Never good at studies—he always poked fun at himself as the class dunce— Cocteau ran away from school and hid out in the casbah of Marseilles until an irate uncle came and hauled him home by the ear. He never did graduate, a source of amusement to him in later years when he lectured at the Collège de France, was offered the Norton Chair in Poetry at Harvard, and was elected to the national academies of France, Belgium, and the United States. The opium addiction, the long sieges in disintoxication clinics, and his homosexual encounters were problems Mme. Cocteau soon learned to close her eyes to. She saw in her son many things to be proud of, including his bravery in World War I, when he volunteered for winter service on the Belgian front and later drove an ambulance through Reims under heavy German bombardment. Luckily, Cocteau's artistic gifts, honed by hard work, also became apparent to her, and she rejoiced in his successes. These were not limited to his own brilliant plays, films, novels, poems, ballets, and journals, but extended to the discovery and promotion of such new young talent as the boy prodigy Raymond Radiguet. Cocteau helped introduce American jazz to Paris, and promoted the composers known as *Les Six*, which included Honegger, Darius Milhaud, Francis Poulenc, and Georges Auric. He met Al Brown, a down-and-out black American boxer who had become a drug addict in Paris, helped rehabilitate him, and saw him regain the bantamweight title.

Far more than grand opera and concert halls, Cocteau's taste ran to the milieu of popular entertainment, the music hall, the circus, and the theater, and these cultural arenas figure in many of his works. The walls of his tiny apartment on the rue de Montpensier in Paris, the first place he could call his own, were covered with scarlet fabric that looked like theater curtains. At the entrance was—and still is—a blackboard with telephone numbers and appointments chalked in his own hand like a backstage theater bulletin board. Cocteau's only real home was the house at Milly-la-Forêt near Fontainebleau, bought jointly in 1947 with his friend Jean Marais, who acted in many of Cocteau's most successful plays and films. This tranquil old house, hidden behind stone walls at the end of a village lane, was a far cry from the wild days at the Hotel Welcome.

Yet, for all the supposed worldliness of his rootless hotel life and the peace of the final contented haven at Milly, it is clear none of these dwellings were where Cocteau really lived. His world was essentially interior, the realm of the imagination. Of the heart. Where his work was. And that was *everywhere*.

Jean Cocteau in Venice, 1947

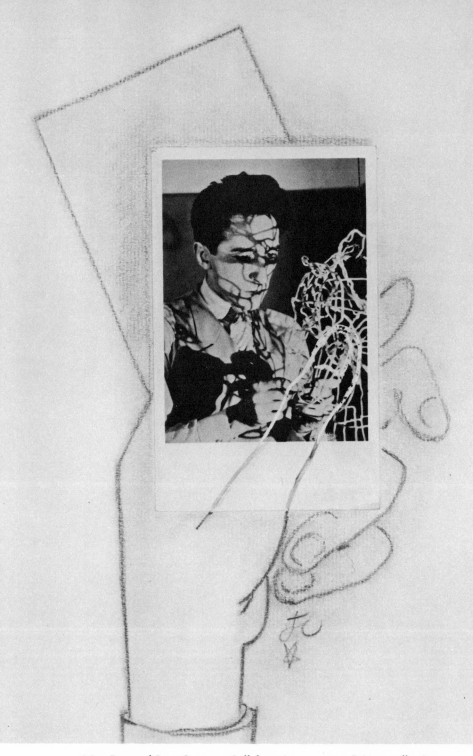

Man Ray and Jean Cocteau. Collaboration, c. 1926. Private collection

Jean Cocteau: 1889–1963

✳ ## A Brief Biography

Francis Steegmuller

O F HIS OWN CAREER Jean Cocteau once said, "Since the age of fifteen I haven't stopped for a minute." Poet, novelist, dramatist, cineast, portraitist; designer of posters, pottery, tapestries, mosaics, neckties, costume jewelry, and of objects executed in glass or fashioned from pipe cleaners—the list of what he called his "transformations" could go on indefinitely. "I have been accused of jumping from branch to branch," he said. "Well, I have—but always in the same tree." He was referring to the tree of poetry. Of all the titles to which he had a claim, he consented to use only one: poet; and that he insisted upon. He was the most self-proclaimed of poets, rigorously classifying all the great variety of his works—poems, novels, plays, essays, drawings, and films—under the headings of "*poésie, poésie de roman, poésie de théâtre, poésie critique, poésie graphique* and *poésie cinématographique*." Even his sculpture was "*poésie plastique*." The insistence could be irritating, and inevitably brought charges of being a "counterfeit" poet. But that slur flies wide of the mark, particularly in one important respect: Cocteau never meant his work to pass as anyone else's, and even when it is imitative it bears a maker's mark that would disqualify any forger: the stamp of a master of paradox and aesthetic epigram, who supplied a unique—and enduring—connection between the classic and the new.

His birthplace itself was special. Maisons-Laffitte, although a suburb of Paris, is not the usual mere bedroom for commuters: its racecourse, its population of splendid horses, with their owners, trainers, and jockeys, and the gala crowds and colors of race days, were among his earliest memories: it was there that he spent childhood summers with his well-to-do bourgeois parents. "Racy," in fact, is not out of place among the many adjectives one can apply to Cocteau and his career.

But his early experiences were also charged with secret tragedy. When he was nine, his father shot himself while lying in bed in the family house in Paris. All that is known of the event is that it took place, in Cocteau's later words, "in circumstances that would not cause anyone to commit suicide today"; and that afterward he himself, for many years, if he had to pass along the rue La Bruyère, "ran through it, hearing and seeing nothing." Beyond that, his father is barely mentioned, and fathers are rare in his writings; when they do appear, they are dim and inglorious. Mothers, on the other hand, are powerful figures. His own had tended to indulge him—a frail child who liked to lie in bed and dress in girl's clothes. Mme. Cocteau was a graceful, conventional woman, quite religious, described by her adoring son as "infallible in matters of honor and morality": she lived, more or less resigned to his many peripeties, until he was in his mid-fifties.

Cocteau began his career, as he said (though his autobiographical writings are as rich in exaggeration as they are in omission), at fifteen—certainly at some point in his teens—by running away from home and school in Paris and spending—he says a year—in the celebrated red-light casbah of Marseilles (deliberately dynamited to rubble by Germans in 1943). Some of his adolescent experiences there are recounted in more or less fictional form in *Le Livre blanc (The White Book)*, a homosexual memoir published anonymously in 1928 and until recently sold, in both French and translations, "under the counter" only. Discovered and brought home by a family emissary, he never returned to school, but began to write verse and to suffer from what he called a lifelong "illness," the "red-and-gold disease" of absorption in the theater. Attractive, witty, and not at all shy, with a precocious ability to make a friend of almost anyone he chose, he was soon haunting both sides of the curtain and was on familiar terms with Parisian stage-folk.

One of these, Edouard de Max, a flamboyant star of the Comédie-Française, sponsored Cocteau—at eighteen—in a series of public and private readings of his charming and ephemeral "salon" poems. Three volumes of these were soon published. And almost as precipitately disowned, never to be reprinted. For Cocteau had experienced the first of what he was later to call his artistic "moultings"—the discarding of old tastes for new. At twenty he discovered a luminous new world, compared with which his own poetic posturing sickened him: the world of Russian ballet.

Traditional Western ballet (as, for example, it is illustrated in the work of Degas) was given a profound aesthetic shock, with results evident to this day, by Serge de Diaghilev's importation to Paris, in 1909, of his company of Russian dancers (who themselves had received a renovating shock a few years earlier from Isadora Duncan, when she first danced in St. Petersburg in 1905). Introduced to Diaghilev by their common friend Misia Sert, Cocteau, nicknamed "Jeanchik" by Diaghilev, became an intimate of the company, attending (often from the wings) performances of *Schéhérazade, Prince Igor, Festin, Les Sylphides,* and the other early productions. He was shrewd enough to express his infatuation with Nijinsky (Diaghilev's particular and personal property) by writing and publishing a six-line poem to the dancer, illustrated by Paul Iribe, which the impresario, although uneasy, had to accept as valuable "publicity." And, commissioned by Diaghilev, Cocteau wrote the scenario for a new ballet, *Le Dieu bleu (The Blue God)*, which, though now best forgotten, was danced by Nijinsky to music by Reynaldo Hahn.

Man Ray. *Jean Cocteau, 1924*

Jean Cocteau. *Memories of the Ballets Russes: Self-Portrait.*
Illustration from *Dessins*, 1924

It was with the Russian ballet that Cocteau began his considerable career as painter and draftsman, a career that was one of
his most engaging aspects (until, in his last decade, it became
pretentious and even pathetic). His first works in this field, in
which he was encouraged by Léon Bakst, the company's chief
costume designer, were a pair of posters, depicting Nijinsky and
Karsavina (he gave the latter his own profile); and soon he was
producing a series of pen-and-ink drawings of backstage scenes
that remain a delightful record of the company's early Paris
seasons. The sensation caused in May 1913 by the first performance of Stravinsky's ballet *Le Sacre du printemps (The Rite of
Spring)*, coupled with the restless Diaghilev's challenge to "Jeanchik" one night as they were walking in the Place de la Concorde—
"Astound me! I'm waiting for you to astound me!"—set off in
Cocteau a desire to "moult" again. He wrote a prose fantasy
which—however Surrealists may disagree—might well be called
premature Surrealism. Entitled *Le Potomak (The Potomac)*, it
aroused general incomprehension. He next besieged Stravinsky
with letters begging him to set to music a new ballet scenario he
was drafting, to be called *David*. But Stravinsky, engrossed in
the composition of *Le Rossignol (The Nightingale)*, was not
responsive.

The outbreak of war in August 1914 changed the world.

It is clear from Cocteau's autobiographical writings that the
horrible years of the first World War were, for him, preeminently
the season of his proudest "moulting"—what he called his move
from Right to Left in the arts: in other words, his penetration of
the artistic avant-garde. As he put it, "There were two fronts:
there was the war front, and then in Paris there was what might
be called the Montparnasse front." By the latter he meant particularly those painters, the Fauves, Cubists, and post-Impressionists
in general, who came to be known collectively as "the School of
Paris." The Cubists, particularly Picasso and Braque, had been
celebrated by the poet Apollinaire in his book *The Cubist Painters* (1913); among the others were the artists Matisse, Vlaminck,
Derain, Modigliani, and Lipschitz. The poets close to them
included Max Jacob and André Salmon; Satie and Varèse were

Jean Cocteau. *Memories of the Ballets Russes: Serge de Diaghilev
and Léon Bakst.* Illustration from *Dessins*, 1924

two of the avant-garde composers. In general, these artists had
had little to do with the Ballets Russes, which they tended to
consider a *divertissement* for fashionable society; and Cocteau
was to become one of the bridges between those artists, that
society, and the Ballets Russes itself. Most important among the
artists for his purpose—he was quick to set himself a definite
goal—were Picasso and Satie.

During the early part of the war he was more active on, or
close to, the other front. Classified as unfit for military service,
he immediately joined a convoy of ambulances organized by
Misia Sert. (Their expeditions to the front near Reims, to bring
wounded to Paris hospitals, were to provide background for
one of his best short novels, *Thomas l'Imposteur [Thomas the
Impostor].*) He edited, illustrated, and largely wrote a short-
lived artistic-patriotic journal, *Le Mot (The Word)*; he met his
first Cubist, Albert Gleizes, who painted his portrait; and an

aviator, the ace Roland Garros, with whom he made several flights and in whose memory he wrote a long poem, *Le Cap de Bonne-Espérance (The Cape of Good Hope)*, in a new, allusive style. Another of his wartime poems, which appeared in *Le Mot* and which he perhaps later thought too traditional and "simple" to add luster to his fame (since he never reprinted it), the beautiful *Quand Nous Serons "Ceux de la Guerre" (When They Call Us "Those Who Went to the War")*, prefigures in an extraordinary way the equally beautiful *Les Lilas et les Roses (Lilacs and Roses)* by Louis Aragon, perhaps the most celebrated poem to come out of France during the second World War. He subsequently joined another ambulance unit founded by Etienne de Beaumont, a wealthy aesthete and sponsor of artists; and this took him first to the maritime front near the Flemish border (which would provide other scenes for *Thomas l'Imposteur*), and later to the bloody battle of the Somme.

It was during these periods of ambulance service, with intervals in Paris, that Cocteau conducted, by correspondence and visit, an energetic courtship of Picasso and Satie, not to mention Diaghilev and Massine—his object being their participation (as designer, composer, producer, and choreographer, respectively) in a new scenario he had written for a ballet, a sequence of turns performed, to attract customers, by a troupe of itinerant vaudevillians outside their caravan. He described it as a "*ballet réaliste*" and called it *Parade*. What he later referred to as "the battle of *Parade*," or sometimes even, characteristically, as "the greatest battle of the war"—a saga of intrigues, cajolings, hectorings, deceptions, compromises, maneuvers of all kinds on the part of everyone concerned—is itself worthy of a ballet scenario. Cocteau won his battle on the afternoon of May 18, 1917, when—after months of preparation, chiefly in Rome, where the Diaghilev company had been spending part of the war—*Parade* was first performed at the Théâtre du Châtelet in Paris. That premiere was an artistic "*scandale*," with vociferous demonstrations by assorted factions in the audience; today, *Parade* has long been regarded as an ancestor, the precursor of much modern "realistic" ballet: in Lincoln Kirstein's phrase, it was the first balletistic "metaphor of the everyday." Audiences at per-

Albert Gleizes. *Study for a Portrait of Jean Cocteau*, 1915–16
Musée National d'Art Moderne, Paris

Picasso and Cocteau, 1955. Collection Edouard Dermit

formances of *Parade* today—delighted by Picasso's curtain and decor, his Cubist carapaces for the Managers, his horse, his costumes for the Chinese Conjurer, the American Girl, and the Acrobats; by Satie's irresistible music; and the swift choreography of Massine—sometimes forget that the concept of the ballet was Cocteau's: *his* presence, after all, is only a name printed in the programme. At the premiere of *Parade*'s first revival in many years, by the Joffrey Ballet in New York on March 22, 1973, there were some who remembered: amid applause for the dancers and producers, voices could be heard from the floor calling for "Cocteau! Cocteau!"—that is, for "Author!"

In 1918, the last year of the war, Cocteau published a little book called *Le Coq et l'Arlequin (The Cock and the Harlequin)*, a celebration of modern music, including American jazz. (He himself was becoming an accomplished drummer. "Stravinsky has lent me his drum," he wrote to his mother—who had reproached him for "wasting his time" playing in a bar he and his friends had founded, called "Le Gaya"—"and I play it as often as I can—I love the instrument for various reasons, poetry not excluded . . . If some kind person should say to you, 'Isn't your son the leader of a Negro jazz band?', please tell them: 'Yes. We think it's the best job he's ever had.'") By this time he was claiming that *Parade* and his writings had earned for him the right to be called a member of the avant-garde. The public regarded him as such, but not so the self-styled "official" avant-garde itself. Dada, founded by Tristan Tzara and others in Zurich in 1916, and anticipated in New York by Marcel Duchamp and Francis Picabia, condescended to Cocteau as an interloper from the bourgeoisie who was emulating their verbal tricks. More savage were the Surrealists, led by André Breton, Louis Aragon, and Philippe Soupault, who began as secessionists from Dada. Many artists, including Picasso, were to look on Cocteau askance, considering him an opportunist in the arts rather than a true creator. Apollinaire seems to have judged him little more than a dandy. There were grounds for those opinions, but Cocteau's postwar career was now to speak for itself.

Throughout the 1920s Cocteau's artistic activity was incessant. Then, as always, he wrote quantities of verse, which was repeatedly collected and published in volumes. This, the "purest" in form of all his varied "poetries," is necessarily the least accessible outside his native tongue. Most of it is not truly translatable, though some translations have been made; let it be said here that much of it is delightful, that it varies greatly in style and in degree of intensity, and that it was Cocteau's particular pride. A number of his poems have been set to music by Poulenc and other composers, and some will be found in anthologies of modern French verse.

Many of his most effective productions called for the collaboration of others, and Cocteau's choice of collaborators was part of his genius. (In this he had perhaps learned much from Diaghilev, for whom he, in turn, would continue to find collaborators.) His promotion of the group of composers called

Les Six—Georges Auric, Louis Durey, Arthur Honegger, Darius Milhaud, Francis Poulenc, and Germaine Tailleferre—included the writing of the scenario for a "spectacle-concert" called *Le Boeuf sur le toit (The Ox on the Roof)*, from the name of a Brazilian samba, *O Boi No Telhado*, to be scored by Milhaud, who had lived in Brazil. It remains one of Milhaud's better-known compositions, although the "spectacle" part is seldom now performed. (A nightclub of the same name, launched by Cocteau in 1922, still exists in Paris.) With friends, Jean Hugo and Roger de la Fresnaye among them, he counterattacked Breton and his cohorts in a newssheet called *Le Coq* (he was always fond of the sound of all or parts of his own name). He fell in love with the precocious sixteen-year-old Raymond Radiguet and encouraged him to write: the rapid result was Radiguet's two novels, *Le Diable au corps (Devil in the Flesh)*, later made into a film starring Gérard Philipe, and *Le Bal du Comte d'Orgel (The Ball of Count d'Orgel)*; and during the brief years of their association Cocteau published two of his best-known novels, *Thomas l'Imposteur*, already mentioned, and *Le Grand Ecart (The Splits)*. A farce-scenario, *Les Mariés de la Tour Eiffel (The Wedding on the Eiffel Tower)*, contains music by all the members of *Les Six* except Louis Durey, and messages recited by Cocteau himself through a megaphone. (*Le Boeuf sur le toit, Les Mariés*, and many more of Cocteau's works exist on recordings.) His adaptation of Sophocles' *Antigone*, with a score by Honegger, scenery by Picasso, and costumes by Gabrielle Chanel, was produced in 1922.

In December 1923, Raymond Radiguet died of typhoid at twenty, and within a few months the shaken Cocteau began to smoke opium. His first five years of addiction and his first several "cures" are the subject of his fascinating notebook, *Opium*, and it was with the aid of the drug that he continued his frenetic professional and social round, always accompanied by maximum publicity. Throughout his career he was one of the most photographed of men: a photographer once remarked to André Maurois, "If I were to take a picture of a village wedding, Jean Cocteau would appear on the film between bride and groom"—a complaint doubly apposite.

Man Ray. *Jean Cocteau and Tristan Tzara*, c. 1922 >

In 1924, at Diaghilev's request, Cocteau helped with the scenarios of two ballets, *Les Biches (The Does)* (score by Poulenc, decor by Marie Laurencin), and *Les Fâcheux (The Woeful)* (score by Auric, decor by Braque), and wrote his own last scenario for Diaghilev, *Le Train bleu* (score by Milhaud, decor by Henri Laurens, and the famous front curtain of two monumental running women by Picasso). His adaptation of *Romeo and Juliet*, with decor by Jean Hugo, was staged that same year, Cocteau himself playing Mercutio. He published a large volume of his intensely witty early drawings, *Dessins*. In 1925, after the first of his opium "cures," proselytized by his Roman Catholic friends Raïssa and Jacques Maritain, he penitently "returned to the sacraments"—reembraced, that is, the Roman Catholicism into which he had been baptized as an infant. This step, too, he publicized, in a *Letter to Jacques Maritain*, accompanied by Maritain's *Reply to Jean Cocteau*; but despite "cure" and "repentance," the opium habit was soon resumed.

On June 15, 1926, his play *Orphée (Orpheus)*, perhaps the most Coctelian of all the dramas, was produced in Paris by the Pitoëffs. (Its later film version is better known today.) It was quickly followed by an exhibition of drawings and "constructions" (some made of pipe cleaners and plaster) called *Poésie plastique—objets, dessins*. In 1927 came his oratorio, *Oedipus Rex*, with Stravinsky's great score; and in 1929 another celebrated and prescient novel, *Les Enfants terribles (The Holy Terrors)* (later a play, and still later a film), and his one-act play for a single character, *La Voix humaine (The Human Voice)*, a monologue spoken into a telephone, probably the most frequently performed of his dramatic works, translated into many languages. Among its performers have been Berthe Bovy at the Comédie-Française, Anna Magnani in Italian on film, Ingrid Bergman in English on recording and on television, Jo Ann Sayers in French on a New York stage, Lillebil Ibsen in Norwegian on a stage in Oslo, and Liv Ullmann in English on the stage in New York. It is also sung to Poulenc's vocal and orchestral score.

For Cocteau the 1930s opened with *Le Sang d'un poète (The*

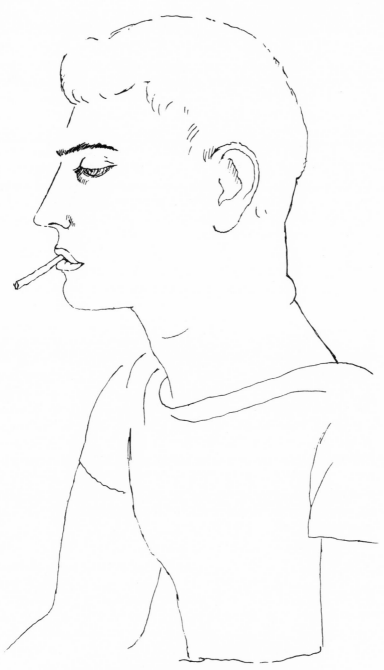

Jean Cocteau. *Portrait of Raymond Radiguet*, 1923
Collection Edouard Dermit

Blood of a Poet), his first film, made in 1930, publicly shown in 1932. (His career as cineast was then deferred, and the decade of the 1930s is notable rather for a series of stage plays, some of them popular successes that greatly enlarged his public and his fame but did not always enhance his artistic reputation—a reputation in turn to be rescued by his subsequent films, some of them created from these plays.) As for *The Blood of a Poet*, though it is now generally accepted as a Surrealist film, it was never conceded by the Surrealists themselves to be truly so. It was the occasion for another vehement attack on Cocteau by Breton and his orthodox followers, who branded it a blatant imitation of what they had officially adopted as the first authentic Surrealist film, Luis Buñuel's *Un Chien andalou*. But the public, including the American film world, have always found *The Blood of a Poet* at least as fascinating as Buñuel's "rival" classic, and it is seldom absent from the screen.

La Machine infernale (The Infernal Machine) (1934), Cocteau's most extended stage version of the Oedipus legend, was produced by Louis Jouvet, with Jean-Pierre Aumont and Jouvet himself in the cast, Cocteau as narrator, and costumes by Christian Bérard. *Les Chevaliers de la table ronde (The Knights of the Round Table)* (1937), a similarly esoteric treatment of the Galahad story, marked the debut in a starring role of an actor destined for popular fame: Cocteau's new protégé, the handsome young Jean Marais. Then came *Les Parents terribles (Intimate Relations)*, with which Cocteau specifically said he intended "to reach the public at large," and which did indeed become his greatest popular stage success. Two more such "successes" followed: *Les Monstres sacrés (The Sacred Monsters)*, and *La Machine à écrire (The Typewriter)*, which caused Eric Bentley to write: "Jean Cocteau seems to me to have become a lost soul. What is disturbing is the awful vacuity of these pieces."

Superior to these mechanical dramas were two volumes of Coctelian journalism: *Portraits-Souvenir (Memory Portraits)*, a series of lively, if not reliable, autobiographical sketches; and *Mon Premier Voyage: Tour du Monde en 80 Jours (My First Journey: Around the World in Eighty Days)*, the episodic travel reportage of a whirlwind (for those days) neo-Jules Verne trip.

This was undertaken for the newspaper *Paris-soir* and, in its American sections, provides amusing glimpses of Harlem, Minsky's Burlesque, and Coney Island. There has recently been published the first volume of his journal beginning in 1951, *Le Passé défini (The Past Definite)*, edited by Pierre Chanel.

The second World War marked as great a turning point in Cocteau's work as had the first.

It was during the macabre years of the German occupation of Paris, from 1940 to 1944, that he most clearly revealed what will always be seen as his greatest weakness—frailty of moral principle. He was no gross collaborator, but the relish he expressed for the "excitement" of the Nazis' arrival, his speedy seeking of the German official license indispensable for the staging of his plays, his sponsoring of an exhibition by Hitler's official sculptor, Arno Breker, can cause little surprise to close observers of his previous career: certain kinds of fortitude were not to be expected of him, while a taste for ultimate novelty in however bizarre a form might be predicted. The picture is blurred by the fact that the "puritanical" Vichy government listed some of his work, particularly *Les Parents terribles* (which was playing in Paris) as "immoral"; and he did express some opposition to its pronouncements. Cocteau and Jean Marais, now his constant companion and an actor in most of his plays, were publicly insulted by Vichyite hoodlums. All of this permitted him to say in later years that during the Occupation he had been "persecuted." However, his manifest willingness to tolerate the company of the occupants brought him to the attention of "purification" tribunals after the Liberation in 1944. He was exonerated of any serious misconduct; and, in a transformation typical of his career, one of his drawings of Marianne in a Liberty Cap, wearing the tricolor rosette of the French Resistance, was disseminated around the world in millions of miniature copies, having been adopted by the Fourth French Republic as its twenty-centime stamp.

During the war years the friendship of Jean Marais was invaluable to Cocteau. Marais helped him master, even if again temporarily, his drug addiction, comforted him on his mother's

Jean Cocteau and Jean Marais

death in 1943, and—stimulated by his own wish to star in films—encouraged Cocteau to return to the medium in which his first venture, *The Blood of a Poet*, had been remarkable and which was peculiarly suited to Cocteau's prescient, mercurial, and phantasmal inventions.

It is scarcely too much to say that Cocteau's artistic importance for the rest of his life, from the last year of the war to his death in 1963, lies almost exclusively in his authorship and production of films; and it is chiefly his films which, particularly outside France, have perpetuated his name: the titles alone conjure up a film festival.

After the gap of over ten years following *The Blood of a Poet*, he resumed his film career with a kind of apprenticeship: the writing of dialogue for a grade-B scenario entitled *Le Baron fantôme (The Phantom Baron)*, directed by Serge de Poligny, with the excellent actress Gabrielle Dorziat (who had appeared in the stage play of *Les Parents terribles*), and with Cocteau himself in the role of the phantom baron of the title. This was followed by the somewhat more sophisticated, but still awkward, *L'Eternel Retour (The Eternal Return)*, a modern-dress version of the Tristan legend, the contemporary Tristan played by Jean Marais (whom the film immediately launched as a screen star), Isolde by Madeleine Sologne, and with a part for Yvonne de Bray, another excellent alumna of *Les Parents terribles*. Then, when for the first time since *The Blood of a Poet* he was enabled to make a film independently, came the poetic and enormously enjoyable *La Belle et la bête (Beauty and the Beast)*, with Josette Day and Jean Marais in his famous "Beast" mask. (The journal Cocteau kept during the making of the film, chronicling the troupe's vicissitudes, the crises, the material shortages of those immediately post-Liberation days, the improvised solutions, the spirit of camaraderie, is almost as delightful as the film itself.)

Next came *L'Aigle à deux têtes (The Eagle with Two Heads)*, very Graustarkian, with Marais, Edwige Feuillère, Georges Aminel (later the first black to be engaged by the Comédie-Française), and a newcomer, Edouard Dermit, who lived with Cocteau as his "adopted" son for the rest of Cocteau's life and became his heir. (As *The Eagle with Two Heads*, this began with

Edouard Dermit and his portrait of Jean Cocteau, Milly-la-Forêt, 1951

brief careers, in English translation and adaptation by Ronald Duncan, on the stages of London and New York, where the presence of Tallulah Bankhead in the cast did not save it from failure. A stage production in Paris also preceded the film.)

Another swashbuckler followed: Victor Hugo's *Ruy Blas*, notable for its Velasquez-like portraits of Spanish grandees. In both films Marais performs spectacular athletic feats in the style of Douglas Fairbanks: by now he was a film idol, with "Jean Marais clubs" organized as far away as Tokyo, where he was known as "the most beautiful Western man."

Les Parents terribles and *Les Enfants terribles* (*The Holy Terrors*) are both skillful, more or less faithful film versions of the plays, whereas *Orphée*, generally considered the finest, the most haunting, of all the films (not least because of the formidable presence of Maria Casarès in the role of Death), transformed the already beautiful play with such power, shifting it into an altogether different realm of drama, that the contrast between the two is often cited as a supreme illustration of the respective possibilities of stage and cinema technique.

The film of *Orphée*, which Cocteau made at the age of sixty, might in the case of another artist be considered the apogee of his career. But as the reader has seen, Cocteau had not one career, but many. (It should perhaps be reiterated that his achievement as a poet "pure and simple"—that is, as a writer of verse—which he claimed to consider his most important, has inevitably been scanted in the present account, due to the difficulties of demonstrating it in a foreign language.) And each of his careers could be said to have enjoyed an apogee of its own. Nevertheless, *Orphée* on film marks a high point, in that the post-Orphée Cocteau, while never silent and far from inconspicuous, was, one might say, less spectacular, less successful in his inventions, less productive of classics, than before. Three of his later works, each in a different genre, require mention here: the short ballet, *Le Jeune Homme et la mort* (*The Young Man and Death*), in which Baryshnikov has recently danced, with Nureyev performing in another recent version on film; the autobiographical volume *La Difficulté d'être* (*The Difficulty of Being*), the most reflective and valid of his works of this kind; and, some think, the volume of "pure" poetry, *Requiem*. His last full-length film, *Le Testament d'Orphée (The Testament of Orpheus)*, toward the making of which François Truffaut contributed the prize money he had won for his film *The Four Hundred Blows*, also has many admirers. But so, alas, do the mural paintings with which Cocteau decorated many a wall, the tapestries, the ceramics, the objects in Venetian glass, and the rest—all of which the present chronicler prefers to leave in decent obscurity.

During his last decade, never out of public view, he was elected to the French Academy, to the Royal Belgian Academy, and was given an honorary doctorate at Oxford. (Of such tributes the younger Cocteau had observed: "The important thing is not to decline an official honor, but not to have deserved it.") W. H. Auden, who received his *honoris causa* at Oxford on the same day as Cocteau, has said of him: "The lasting feeling that his work leaves is one of happiness; not of course in the sense that it excludes suffering, but because, in it, nothing is rejected, resented or regretted."

Jean Cocteau lived to be seventy-two, cared for at the end by Jean Marais, and by his "adopted" son, Edouard Dermit. His intimates agreed that "he never seemed old"; and when he died, to the accompaniment of the usual publicity, in 1963, one can imagine him saying of that supreme event, which came in the form of a heart attack, that it was merely the last, and grandest, of his "moultings."

Jean Cocteau and W. H. Auden at Oxford, 1956

Jacques-Emile Blanche. *Portrait of Jean Cocteau*, 1912.
Musée des Beaux-Arts, Rouen

A Native Son of Paris

Roger Shattuck

IN THE WINTER OF 1904–05 two journalists for *Gil Blas* inter-viewed—in person or by letter—ninety-seven French and Bel-gian writers. During its piecemeal appearance in the Paris news-paper, the survey provoked enough interest to earn publication by the distinguished house that represented many of the authors interviewed.[1] To the inevitable questions about "the dominant tendency" in literature at the moment and about the shape of things to come, the eminent writers answered with a lengthy, uninspired mishmash of Naturalism, Symbolism, revived classi-cism, and new social concerns. They commented without heat on the importance of "schools" to organize and activate the literary scene. The only subject they disagreed about with any real vehemence was free verse—its contribution to poetry and its chances of survival. (The nays had it.) Explicitly or by their listless tone, they all bore witness to the stagnant condition of French letters after the decline of Naturalism and Symbolism and after the wrenchings of the Dreyfus affair. The most influential figures, Anatole France and Maurice Barrès, had little to say. Gide and Claudel, among the youngest interviewed, succumbed to the generally mournful tone. Valéry, Proust, Jarry, Apollinaire, and Bergson, all of them active, were neither interviewed nor mentioned in the 400 pages of literary trivia. It looked like a dead calm.

We know now, of course, how fast the rebound came in the arts and literature. The Fauves—with the Douanier Rousseau cast into the same cage—were identified and named in the fall of 1905, and pushed Impressionism further into the past. Within four to five years Cubism became the most dynamic new movement in painting, and Diaghilev captured *le tout Paris* with his Russian operas and ballets. At the same time Gide's and Copeau's new literary review, *La Nouvelle Revue Française*, signaled the entry of a new generation of writers, and in 1912 Apollinaire's review, *Les Soirées de Paris*, gave the avant-garde painters and poets their own lively organ. What burst forth between 1905 and 1914 in Paris was a dynamic compound of renewed classicism, unbridled experimentation, cool scientific nihilism, and a rash of primitive devices and attitudes derived from African, Oceanic, folk, and ancient sources, as well as from the art of children and the insane. Particularly in the prewar seasons of Les Ballets Russes, these manifestations found an enthusiastic public ready to be astonished and to respond. The artistic impetus that arose in the first decade of the century carried right through World War I to spawn Dada and Surrealism and the experiments of the 1920s. It required the political and social preoccupations of the 1930s to slow it and divert it. The avant-garde of the early twentieth century in Paris thrived as much in the traditional institutions of salon, theater, and café as in the more recent institutions of cabaret and cinema. All of them increasingly fostered collaboration among the arts, subject to no established hierarchy. In their survey Le Cardonnel and Vellay had consulted the wrong oracles.

Many of the greatest participants in this upsurge of activity in Paris were foreigners—Picasso, Apollinaire, Stravinsky, Arp, Stein, de Chirico, Man Ray, Ernst. The cordial welcome they all ultimately received points up an irony about one certified native son of Paris, Jean Cocteau. Intimately identified with this juncture in the arts—it was chronologically, geographically, culturally, temperamentally, and aesthetically his own—Cocteau nevertheless could not ever feel easy and secure at its shifting center. Probably he was too close, had too many advantages. Some fate or trait debarred him from unqualified admission to his own rightful domain. Still, he flourished for half a century in Paris and left an important mark in several arts. All these circumstances have made Cocteau one of the most revealing artistic and historical figures of that remarkable era.

Cocteau was brought up in the heart of Paris, between the Boulevard Haussmann and Pigalle. An acute sense of fashion in all things, of the theatricality of life, and of the fickleness of the public, highbrow and lowbrow, came to him very early from his hot-house environment. *"La comédie est fort avancée"* (The play is far advanced) was the way he expressed the idea of getting older.

Cocteau was also both helped and hampered by having too many talents. A prolific writer in every known genre, he tells us that the formal act of sitting down at a desk stopped his flow of words. Consequently he wrote anywhere, anytime, on his lap, unstintingly. From the start he was a nonstop conversationalist, or rather monologuist. Anna de Noailles—a close friend in private—refused to see him in public for fear he would out-talk her. Drawing and design apparently came naturally to him, sometimes with pleasing results. His grandfather's collection of Stradivarius instruments and his family's familiarity with scores and concerts gave him an easy entrée into the world of music and musicians. Some undefined combination of talents made it possible for Cocteau to become a serious filmmaker, as both author and director, after the age of fifty. From the start he was endowed with a vivacious disposition and compulsive intelligence that enabled him to form friendships with people from all walks of life. Others, reacting against his social connections and public posturing, considered him an incorrigible *arriviste*. Gide painted an unsympathetic portrait of him as Robert de Passavant (Windbreaker) in *The Counterfeiters*.

We distrust extreme versatility. We nod wisely on hearing

Jean Cocteau

that the universally gifted Leonardo could never properly finish
any task. Cocteau aroused immediate suspicion because he
always played the child prodigy who knows too much too soon
and cannot grow up or grow old without loss of face. Charlatanry
cannot be far off; yet the accomplishments are many, and some
of them lasting. All in all, Cocteau presents a complex figure. It
is appropriate and inevitable that one of the most probing
accounts of his life and art can be found in Frederick Brown's
unsparing biography, *An Impersonation of Angels*.

My own introduction to Cocteau's work has helped me come
to terms with his many shapes. In the spring of 1947 I went to
Paris as a young man with a commission from Ezra Pound to
carry out two errands. I was to hunt down the sculptor Brancusi
and report on his health and work—a story for another occasion.
And I was to obtain a copy of Cocteau's latest book of poetry,
La Crucifixion, and send it to Pound at St. Elizabeth's Hospital.
At the same time I came upon the short volume of essays, *La
Difficulté d'être (The Difficulty of Being)*. Up to that time
Cocteau had been little more to me than a name. Now I discovered two of his most striking and successful works. Four
years later, while conducting me through the magnificent ruins
of ancient Thebes near modern Luxor where he was in charge of
French excavations, the brilliant Egyptologist Alexander Varille
told me that one visitor had understood that the only way to
"translate" the laminated meanings of hieroglyphics into a contemporary idiom would be by means of film. That man was Jean
Cocteau, who had visited these same sites only a few months
earlier. His eye had encompassed the subtle interrelations of
inscriptions, architecture, landscape, season, Nile level, the
heavens, and cosmic juncture. No system of writing as we know
it can register all that information. Cocteau had proposed that a
series of films could begin to do justice to it. It is perhaps this
kind of overreaching, unitary vision that induced Cocteau to
classify everything he produced as "poetry."

In the dazzling versatility of his career, however, his poetry—
as opposed to his "plastic poetry," "cine poetry," and so forth—is
perhaps in danger of being overlooked. Somewhat unexpectedly,
this pursuer of fame and fashion could produce poetry that com-

bines verbal agility approaching playfulness with genuine spiritual urgency. Before sending *The Crucifixion* to Pound, I read its twenty-five short stanzas. Without resolving the poem's enigma, the last stanza displays its pulse and several of its themes.

25

A genoux à droite
et à gauche. Seul hélas
de mon espèce (il n'y a pas de quoi
être fier) sous une cotte
de maille faite en chiffres sous
une armure de vacarme
seule à genoux à gauche
à droite—la neige aux mains d'aveugle
mettant la nappe—je ferme
à genoux seul de mon espèce
hélas dans cette chambre où le crime
eût lieu la bouche
jaune de ma savante
blessure capable
de prononcer quelques mots.

———————

Kneeling to right
and left. Alone alas
of my own kind (nothing here
to quicken pride) beneath a coat
of monogrammed and ciphered mail beneath
a clanking suit of armor
kneeling alone to left
and right—blind-handed snow
spreading the altar cloth—I close
kneeling alone of my own kind
alas in this room where the crime
took place the yellow
mouth of my knowing
wound just able
to pronounce these words.

Cocteau has written a rhythmic chant for a personal reenactment of an unrepeatable and ever-present event. His conversion to Catholicism under the influence of Jacques Maritain and their public exchange of letters do not pertain here. The poem uses a flat diction and repetitive structure to transform familiarity into mystery. It is one of the least typical and most convincing of Cocteau's writings.

One other aspect of Cocteau's talent I wish to recognize is as well known as the first is neglected.

"The Truth is too naked; she does not inflame men."

"Victor Hugo was a lunatic who thought he was Victor Hugo."

"Nothing is more difficult than to sustain a bad reputation."

"The tact of audacity consists in knowing how far to go too far."

"The Louvre is a morgue; you go there to identify your friends."

"Living is a horizontal fall."

Cocteau's adeptness in coining a *boutade* or quip at the proper moment—in conversation or in writing—goes a long way toward explaining his public success. Effortlessly, it seemed, he could advertise with one-liners whatever he did, whether he was managing the comeback of a bantam-weight boxer, or adapting a Greek tragedy with Stravinsky, or helping to launch a new night spot. His skill at reducing ages of wisdom to the dimensions of a maxim loaded with paradox and irony corresponds to the sense of *velocity* that made Cocteau run. The film *The Blood of a Poet* is framed, start and finish, by successive shots of a factory chimney collapsing—stock trope for instantaneity or simultaneity. But the device seems to belong to Cocteau as his own, without cuteness or contrivance. For in his universe everything is going on at once, breathlessly, at cross-purposes or with miraculous harmony, the way he glimpsed it in the ruins at Thebes, the way he reveals it in his films.

In work after work Cocteau tells us that it is very difficult to exist, above all because we don't know how to attune ourselves to our most precious and ominous gift: time. He never conquered that difficulty, but he lived closer to it than most.

1. Georges Le Cardonnel and Charles Vellay, *La Littérature contemporaine, Opinions des écrivains de ce temps*, Mercure de France, 1905.

Jean Cocteau

Cocteau and His Times: An Intellectual Backdrop

✳

Doré Ashton

> *Père Ubu: Cornegidouille! Nous n'aurons point tout démoli si nous ne démolissons même les ruines! Or je n'y vois d'autre moyen que d'en équilibrer de beaux édifices bien ordonnés.*
>
> Father Ubu: Cornegidouille! We won't have demolished everything if we don't destroy even the ruins. But I don't see any other way except to balance things out with some beautiful, well-constructed buildings.
>
> —Alfred Jarry,
> epigraph for *Ubu enchaîné* (*1900*)

EVEN before the curtain rose on *Le Sacre du printemps (The Rite of Spring)* on May 31, 1913, the hall already echoed with whistles, catcalls, applause, and ironic bravos. Stravinsky had produced a stunning "event" of a kind long appreciated in France. The story of modernism in France is punctuated by such events, sometimes played out in public, as in the 1830 riot over Victor Hugo's play—known ever since as "The Battle of *Hernani.*" Sometimes these events only registered on and were nurtured by the small circles of passionate avant-gardists. But the explosion of *Le Sacre*, with its ecstatic rhythms that made Debussy describe it as "an extraordinary, ferocious thing," seemed to many, even at the time, an "event" that would reverberate in history. Certainly it charged the young Jean Cocteau with a new mission. In its "savage sadness," its "noises of farm and camp," its "little melodies that arrive from the depth of centuries," Cocteau saw "Georgics of prehistory" and understood Stravinsky's importance.

There had been many avatars of the "ferocious" ballet. Attraction to the primitive had already been apparent in the eighteenth and nineteenth centuries, expressed in stereotyped images of the "noble savage." Primitivism found increasing numbers of fervid advocates during the last troubled decade of the nineteenth century. Paul Gauguin argued strenuously for a reinterpretation of the notion of "savage," sarcastically remarking in his journals that Europeans saw Maori works of art as "savage" when in fact they were refined and beautiful. At the same time, Nietzsche was enlightening the French, helping them to perceive the Dionysiac as well as the Apollonian in art. André Gide absorbed the message in *Les Nourritures terrestres (The Fruits of the Earth)*, published in 1897. In his essays Gide spoke passionately of Nietzsche's wrecking procedures; the philosopher, he observed, demolished ferociously but "nobly, gloriously, superhumanly, like a new, violent conqueror of old things." "Yes," Gide wrote in 1898, "to speak well of Nietzsche one needs more passion than schooling . . . every great creator, every great affirmer of Life is neccessarily a Nietzschean."

Rimbaud's ringing question, "What if?" had awakened a wild need to break the mold of conventional culture. The subjectivism apparent in the poetry and painting of the Symbolist movement reflected Rimbaud's quasi-scientific question, and found support in the newly published works of such scientists of the mind as Jean-Martin Charcot, whose studies of hysteria stirred wide interest, and Pierre Janet, whose *L'Automatisme psychologique*, published in 1889, gave currency to the word "subconscious." Increasingly, scientists and philosophers associated the subconscious with acts of the imagination. (In 1897, for example,

Pablo Picasso. *Portrait of Stravinsky*, 1920. Musée Picasso, Paris

one Paul Chamoneix published *Cerebral Physiology: The Subconscious in Artists, Savants, and Writers*.) Janet had written respectfully about "hysterics" who were seers, prophets, and geniuses. His boyhood friend, Henri Bergson, had spoken in *Matter and Memory*, published in 1896, of a *fonction fabulatrice* and had advanced his theory of the primacy of intuition in the events of mental life.

Ferocious, earthy, intuitive, individualistic—such epithets occurred frequently in late-nineteenth-century reflections. But so did such words as spiritual, abstract, transcendental, and sublime. A kind of apocalyptic purism flourished, led by the gently uncompromising Stéphane Mallarmé. The poet himself became a mysterious center of thought through which passed such diverse spirits as Gide, Gauguin, and Valéry. Yet, for all the otherworldliness of many fin-de-siècle poets and painters, most "were anarchists with all the altruism of their hearts," as John Rewald has written. They sanctioned such acts of violence as the violent bombings perpetrated by Ravachol and Vaillant. Even the mild and ethereal Mallarmé referred to these anarchists as "those saints." Political passions rose unusually high among artists, particularly during the Dreyfus affair. Maurice Barrès, who had been admired for his prose style, suddenly became anathema to many of his confreres when, in 1897, he published *The Uprooted*, a novel advocating a nationalism that he later put into action within an exceedingly distasteful political context of antiintellectualism and racism. However, for every Rightist among artists and intellectuals, there were dozens of opponents who identified the struggle against reactionary politics with the struggle against philistinism, their greatest enemy since the revolution of 1830.

The need to demolish through creating, heralded by Alfred Jarry's *Père Ubu*, remained a constant in French modernist thought. It was a particularly urgent principle during the years preceding the first World War. This period of flourishing "isms" rapidly, breathlessly, and with tremendous vitality brought the motifs of fin-de-siècle rebellion to their apogee. Artists set about to demolish "even the ruins." The prewar period was in turn a rehearsal for postwar tendencies in which the historicizing attitude that saw "events" as the propagators of art was reconfirmed. The hunger for a *frisson nouveau*, so evident among the so-called decadents of the fin-de-siècle, had not abated. And there were many new sensations to come.

Some of them were kindled by painters only too willing to *épater le bourgeois* in a stunning series of public scandals, beginning with the 1905 exhibition of the works of Matisse, Derain, Vlaminck, and others. These paintings called down the wrath of the critics, who referred to the artists as *"Les Fauves."* Soon Matisse's daring departure from the conventions of naturalistic color (although this departure logically followed from Symbolism) and his willingness to find his "arabesque" by nearly abstract means stirred the public to frenzies of outrage. Not long after, the poet Guillaume Apollinaire—loquacious, energetic, and sensitive to the most diverse currents—began his campaign for "the new spirit." Taking up Baudelaire's demand for surprise as the hallmark of the new, Apollinaire allowed himself to be surprised in his numerous journalistic essays by some of the strongest figures of the day, among them Pablo Picasso and Georges Braque, whose formal explorations won them the scornful title of Cubists. Apollinaire himself added to the flurry of "isms" by inventing "Orphism," a term largely manufactured to cover the color experiments of his friend Robert Delaunay. Apollinaire was also prescient enough to discern the metaphysical aspects of Giorgio de Chirico, whom he first noticed in 1912. The prevailing ravenous appetite for intellectual excitement can be gauged not only in Apollinaire's ebullient chronicles, but also by the fact that a distinguished newspaper like *Le Figaro* would prominently display the Futurist Manifesto in 1909, in which Marinetti declared that "There is no longer beauty except in the struggle. No more masterpieces without an aggressive character. Poetry must be a violent assault against the unknown forces in order to overcome them and prostrate them before men."

Apollinaire, along with his friends Max Jacob and Blaise Cendrars, was doing his best to change the character of French poetry. Turning away from the lofty tone of the Symbolists, these poets and others injected irony, burlesque, ordinary conversation, and unorthodox syntax into their works, assaulting

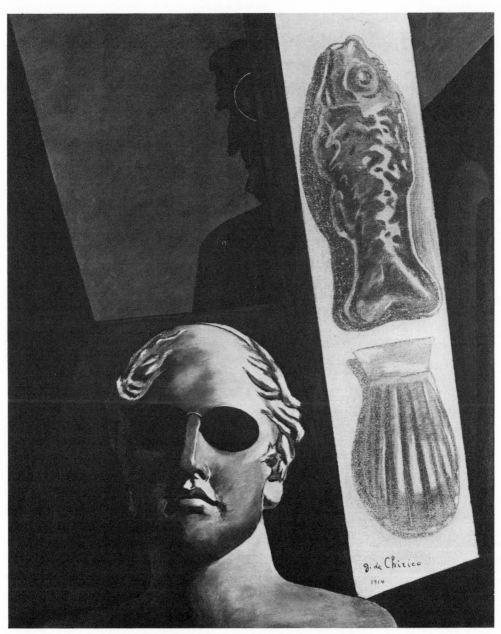

Giorgio de Chirico. *Portrait of Guillaume Apollinaire*, 1914
Musée National d'Art Moderne, Paris

the citadels of French tradition in the interest of the new. To strengthen their hand they formed alliances with painters, and when appropriate, championed other artists who seemed to be flouting public taste. They formed a natural audience for such avant-garde events as the staging of Raymond Roussel's *Impressions of Africa* in 1912. This was an event vividly remembered by the young Marcel Duchamp, who delighted in the absurdities of the tale of Frenchmen shipwrecked in Africa and subjected to the cruel mechanical fantasies of an inventor-king. They were also on hand to cheer the reemergence after 1910 of Erik Satie, who described himself as "the strangest musician of our time."

The painters had called attention to the old ideal of the primitive, the exotic, in their enthusiasm for African and Oceanic art. A still more public example of the taste for the exotic was the phenomenal success of Diaghilev's Ballets Russes, which made its first appearance in Paris in 1909. The sumptuous colors that Léon Bakst and Alexandre Benois used in their sets and costumes overwhelmed Paris. As Benois wrote:

> It was Russian culture that triumphed in Paris. . . . Our primitive wildness, our simplicity revealed itself in Paris as something more refined, developed, and subtle than the French themselves could do.
>
> The success of the ballets is based on the fact that Russians are still capable of believing in their creations, that they still retain enough spontaneity to become absorbed, just as children are completely absorbed in their play, in the God-like play which is art. This secret has been lost on the Western stage, where everything is technique, everything is artificiality, and from which have gradually disappeared the mysterious charm of self-oblivion, the great Dionysiac intoxication, the driving force of art.

With the next season's performance of *Schéhérazade*, the Ballets Russes entered the public consciousness. Even dress designers like Paul Poiret were inspired by Bakst's rich colors and folkloric designs to create new fashions, including "harem pajamas." The Dionysiac intoxication with the Russians reached its climax in 1913 with *Le Sacre du printemps*, the "great insult to habit" that turned Jean Cocteau away from what he called "the soft cushion of Orientalism."

World War I did not seem to slacken the pace of vanguard

events. They continued to occur with staccato regularity, even magnifying prewar trends. Although certain sectors in the arts had been stirred by Jules Romains's humanistic *"unanisme,"* and were determinedly pacifist, others entered the war with a certain exhilaration, at least at the beginning. Nietzsche had predicted that the art of the future would be spectacle. Cocteau, among others, was determined to carry out that prophecy, and the theater was its natural arena. A perennial conducting wire, Cocteau was expert at appropriating past currents and charging them with spectacular energy. He quickly caught up with the experimental voices of Apollinaire and Cendrars, abandoned his own refined exoticism, and in his zeal to astonish, brought to fruition an old aesthetic ideal, the *Gesamtkunstwerk (Total Art Work).*

The French had been flirting with Wagner's ideas since the mid-nineteenth century. Baudelaire wrote extensively and fervently about Wagner's new aesthetic, quoting with admiration his letter to Berlioz in which he spoke of "an alliance of all the arts uniting in a common object, which was the creation of the most perfect, the only true art work." Baudelaire envisioned "a coincidence of several arts" that would be more than the standard opera or ballet or theater piece, and Cocteau saw the way to do it. In the ballet *Parade*, he was to extend the tradition that had drawn Toulouse-Lautrec to the popular music halls and Picasso and his friends to the Cirque Médrano.

Cocteau's instinct was sure; he met Picasso in 1916 and learned from him that a ditty sung by a street-singer, if one knows how to listen to it, may prove more rewarding than *Götterdämmerung*. From Satie, Cocteau learned that "in our age, the greatest audacity is simplicity." While listening to Satie's *Pieces in the Shape of a Pear*, he was inspired with the idea of *Parade*. Some of his notions had already been formulated when he first met the painter Albert Gleizes, with whom he had planned a radical production of *A Midsummer Night's Dream* to be performed at the Cirque Médrano with the famous clowns, the Fratellini Brothers, among the actors. This unrealized earlier project had already heralded a fusion of all the arts. Newly introduced to revolutionary trends in music, Cocteau meant to use a medley

Francis Picabia. *Erik Satie*, 1924. Musée de la Danse, Stockholm

of vanguard compositions, among them Satie's *Gymnopédies*, and to have the composer Edgar Varèse conduct it. Varèse had spent many prewar hours in the cafés of Montparnasse with such companions as Picasso, Apollinaire, and André Salmon. While still a student he had discovered Helmholtz's writings on perception, and, curious about Helmholtz's experiments with sirens, had bought two of them with which he proceeded to make "beautiful parabolas and hyperboles of sound." It was through Varèse that Cocteau met Picasso.

Writing to Stravinsky on April 11, 1916, Cocteau called Picasso a "sentimental mandolinist and fierce picador," and described Satie as "an old angel who conceals the fact that he is only twenty." He told Stravinsky that the piece would be ready in October, and added: "May it distill all the involuntary emotion given off by circuses, music halls, carrousels, public halls, factories, seaports, the movies, etc. etc." Picasso's enthusiasm for the project of *Parade* had kindled slowly, but eventually he capitulated, boldly moving beyond the bohemia of Montmartre and Montparnasse, which had resolutely shunned the Ballets Russes as decadent entertainment for *le tout Paris*. His decision (probably abetted by depression over the absence of his friends who were at the front and by the death of his mistress), was profoundly to affect the course of the visual arts in France. As *chef d'école* of the uncompromising Cubists, his defection (as his colleagues thought of it) was a momentous matter; Picasso himself came to think of his own entry into the world of spectacle as a break with his aesthetic past. The composer Poulenc quotes him at the railroad station, where he was about to leave for Italy with Cocteau, saying, "Long life to our followers! It's thanks to them that we look for something else."

Parade was indeed something else. Picasso's contribution—above all, the great Cubist sculptures that pretended to be costumes—stunned the audience. His long-standing interest in burlesque had found a perfect outlet. Satie's music, "so simple, so raw, so naively intricate, shocked everybody by its breeziness," wrote Poulenc. "For the first time—it has happened often enough since, God knows—the music hall was invading art with a capital A. A one-step is danced in *Parade!* When *that* began, the audience let loose with boos and applause . . ." The riotous event brought the wounded Apollinaire to the fore, brandishing his bandage and uniform to quell angry theater patrons. (He had written the program note, in retrospect an important document, since he had used the word "Surrealism" to characterize the union of arts "which heralds the advent of a more complete art.") Apollinaire himself would soon succumb to the appeal of spectacle in *Les Mamelles de Tirésias (The Breasts of Tiresias)*, his rollicking, proto-Surrealist play performed shortly before his death in 1918. The gradual entry of the absurd into modern French life and letters, as well as the new emphasis on the "real" (by which the artists seemed to mean the life of ordinary people and their entertainments), was given impetus through these theatrical events.

Upheavals in literary life were also in the making. Two young soldiers, André Breton and Louis Aragon, who regarded Apollinaire as a model, wrote to him from their military posts. In Switzerland, the Dadaists were looking back to Jarry, Apollinaire, Roussel, and Nietzsche. Tristan Tzara, who would soon bring Dada to Paris, was already in touch with Apollinaire, Cendrars, Modigliani, Picasso, Jacob, and Reverdy, all of whom appeared in the Zurich *Dada* magazine. Several little magazines sprang up during the war. The most significant was edited by Pierre Reverdy, a poet who had frequented Picasso's circle. Reverdy founded *Nord-Sud (North-South)* in 1917. The following year he published a manifesto, *The Image*, which was to provide subsequent Surrealists with rich resources. He wrote that the image is a pure creation of the mind. "It cannot be born from a comparison, but from two realities, more or less distant, brought together." Young poets and artists such as Duchamp knew exactly what he meant.

The war effectively demolished the old order in almost every phase of life. "Like a kaleidoscope which is now and then given a turn, society arranges successively in different orders elements which one would have supposed to be immovable, and composes a fresh pattern," wrote Marcel Proust. After the war, the clear divisions in the human comedy were no longer discernible. Countesses and painters, stockbrokers and poets and even clerks met on the neutral ground of the café or theater. Life was kaleidoscopic. Although few recognized it, the Russian revolution had set the scene for profound change. It was often artists who responded most exuberantly to the new possibilities. Although many simply picked up where they had left off in 1914, there were others who sought, as Picasso said, something else.

As they had before the war, French writers tended to cluster around little magazines. The influential group around Gide that had founded the prewar *Nouvelle Revue Française* regrouped, with Jacques Rivière as editor. His opening statement, in 1919, reflected a resurgence of national pride in the French gifts of clarity and intellect. He attacked romanticism and announced "We shall describe what seems to us to foreshadow a classical renaissance . . . a deep, inner classicism . . . We shall welcome the claims of the intellect, which today is obviously endeavoring to recover its rights in art; not in order to replace feeling entirely, but to analyse it, to rule over it." Rivière's appeal to the intellect was balanced by the equally passionate appeal to feeling by the founders of *Littérature*, André Breton, Louis Aragon, and Philippe Soupault. They welcomed Dada internationalism, which the *NRF* had attacked, and soon Breton and Soupault began publishing fragments of their collaborative work, *Les Champs magnétiques (Magnetic Fields)*, produced, they claimed, entirely through automatic writing.

In the visual arts, classicism, or at least realism, had made inroads, although the towering example of Picasso was not as retrograde as many thought. Already during the war he had amused himself by drawing a portrait of Max Jacob in a manner reflecting Ingres. His associations with the milieu of the high bourgeoisie through Diaghilev were thought to have influenced him in his new classical mood, although after his marriage to Olga Koklova (a ballerina in the Ballets Russes) he wrote wistfully from fashionable Biarritz to Apollinaire about his old bohemian life. Apollinaire answered, shortly before his death: "The poems I am writing now will enter more easily into your present preoccupations. I try to renew poetic style, but in a classical rhythm." Picasso's work during 1919 included drawings based on classical mythology. He then progressed to monumental female figures modeled in full chiaroscuro. But he did not give himself over entirely to the prevailing return to order. At the same time he was making his great classical figure composition, *Three Women at the Spring*, he was working on an equally classic group of Cubist paintings, including the two versions of *The Three Musicians*. Later, when his friends formed the Surrealist group, Picasso showed them the provocative objects he had made from burlap, cardboard, and nails. These were subsequently reproduced in the journal *La Révolution surréaliste*. Perhaps the strongest reminder that Picasso's classicism was but one of his many masks is the superb painting from 1925, *The Three Dancers*, in which three distorted bodies closely packed into the space of a Parisian apartment perform a violent faran-

Pablo Picasso. *Self-Portrait*, 1917. Musée Picasso, Paris

Pablo Picasso. *Olga Koklova*, 1917. Musée Picasso, Paris

dole. Jagged edges, high-pitched colors, a disquieting frenzy, plus a looming black profile, combine to give this painting an Expressionist furor that was infinitely remote from his classical works.

Matisse, who had produced some of his most austere and strikingly abstracted paintings during the early years of the war (*The Piano Lesson*, for instance), moved into a period of relatively tranquil descriptive paintings that in their ease and calm reflected a shift in spirit much in keeping with the times. There had been calls for a "return to the object," and André Derain, just after the war, was invoking the classical masters, beginning with Raphael. "Only Raphael is divine," he wrote in *L'Esprit nouveau* in 1920. A revival of figure painting brought with it a renewed interest in both Courbet and Corot. The avant-garde hastily lowered its sights to include the whole French realist tradition. Brancusi, who in the 1920s was often to be seen in the cafés and bars favored by advanced artists, contributed too to the spirit of a new classicism, remarking, "Simplicity is not an end in art, but one arrives at simplicity in spite of oneself, in approaching the real sense of things."

Realism and classicism were not necessarily synonymous. For Cocteau, in fact, the margins between them were very wide. The exuberance of *Parade* had released his high sense of fun and confirmed him in his quest for the "real" among the popular entertainments that would become so fashionable during the roaring twenties. In 1918 he published *Le Coq et l'Arlequin (The Cock and the Harlequin)*, a rambling essay in which he launched his campaign for the new music of *Les Six*, largely by singing the praises of Satie, who "clears, simplifies, and strips rhythm naked." Within months, Cocteau was at work pushing his notion of a simplified poetic theater in the "spectacle-concert" based on Darius Milhaud's composition *Le Boeuf sur le toit (The Ox on the Roof)*. Cocteau wanted "to give the impression of improvisation but with nothing left to chance." The poetry that he maintained was endemic to theater was to be pure: "*Parade* still had a literary content, a message. Here I avoid subject and symbol. Nothing happens, or what does happen is so crude, so ridiculous, that it is as though nothing happens.

Look for no double meaning, no anachronism in the *Boeuf . . .*"
The Boeuf was set in an American bar, reflecting the rage for
things American that swept Paris during the 1920s. At the same
time, Paris was discovering a new voice, greatly amplified thanks
to Cocteau, in the young prodigy, Raymond Radiguet. This adolescent rebel, who captivated so many French intellectuals, came
forward with a stern doctrine that he called *"le conformisme
anti-conformiste."* He scorned the modern obsession with originality, and before he was twenty wrote *Devil in the Flesh* in an
unencumbered style that stressed the French tradition of objec-
tive clarity. Radiguet's emergence on the literary scene not only
reflected modern France's cyclical fascination with youth, it also
marked a triumphant French entry into the Americanized world
of publicity. Balzac had already analyzed the impact of industri-
alization on literature in *Lost Illusions*, but he could hardly have
imagined the strategies for creating a bestseller that began in the
1920s. The publisher Bernard Grasset had immediately seen the
possibilities in advertising his child genius as the equal of
Rimbaud. He sent proofs to forty-one critics with a blurb written by Cocteau and Radiguet emphasizing the link between the
two young writers. He arranged for the distribution of a film
showing "the youngest novelist in France" signing his contract.
Some thirty reviews of the book and a sale of 40,000 copies
during the first year rewarded his efforts. This was an "event"
that set new criteria for the success of an aesthetic idea, and one
that marked a shift in attitudes toward the erstwhile "alienated"
artists.

During the 1920s Paris, and especially Montparnasse, became a
magnet for disaffected artistic spirits from all over the world. It
was a great era for expatriates, lost-generation idealists, naive
seekers of aesthetic panaceas, and even for the indigenous
bohemians who made the rounds of the cafés providing local
color in exchange for free drinks. The hard-drinking tradition
established by Modigliani and Soutine did not inhibit serious
conversation among artists and writers from many nations, nor
did it prevent exuberant brawling, often undertaken in the name
of one or another school of artistic thought. Cocteau and many

Man Ray. *Raymond Radiguet*, 1921

of his friends saw Paris as an agora, a public place, and Montparnasse as a country in which everyone was patriotic to art. For him, and for certain of his favored artistic friends, "politics didn't exist."

But for others, the most serious disturbances were erupting in public life, not in the life of art. An undercurrent of uneasiness accompanied the most ebullient spirits. There was a lot to be uneasy about. In 1922 Mussolini marched on Rome, and in 1923 the French occupied the Ruhr. There was a fascist coup in Spain. Hitler made his first Putsch in Munich. Two years later the French were embroiled in a police action in Morocco that was thoroughly alarming to bohemia. The gaiety of the Jazz Age was not unmitigated.

Those who proved especially responsive to troubling public events were the Surrealists, who after Breton's manifesto of October 1924 consolidated themselves, if only for a time. Their journal, *La Révolution surréaliste*, began with a broad, internationalist anarchic vision. They did not want merely to create art; they wished nothing less than to transform the world, as Marx had suggested. To the achievement of such a monumental task, all petty concerns such as the aesthetic value of a work had to be subjugated. Surrealism, finally, was to be experienced as a new metaphysics, a new poetics, and an entirely new apparatus for living. As the world began slipping toward the disaster that would be World War II, Breton and some of his cohorts sought a more political dimension. They undertook a series of rapidly shifting political alliances that one writer likened to a mad tea party. But even with their volatile politics, the Surrealists remained faithful to certain premises. They continued to stress the significance of Freud. They insisted on an international rather than a national literature. They celebrated such adolescent forebears as Rimbaud and Lautréamont. And they advocated a spiritual freedom that no political creed could limit. (Some of their positions were not so eccentric. Their exaltation of youthful geniuses coincided with the republication of Gide's *The Fruits of the Earth* in 1923 and again in 1926, and their emphasis on contingency and chance matched the excitement in other camps over Gide's *acte gratuite* from *Lafcadio's Adventures*, also

Man Ray. *Surrealist Checkerboard* (left to right: André Breton, Max Ernst, Salvador Dali, Hans Arp, Yves Tanguy, René Clair, René Creve, Paul Eluard, Giorgio de Chirico, Alberto Giacometti, Tristan Tzara, Picasso, René Magritte, Victor Brauner, Benjamin Péret, G. Rosey, Joan Miró, E. L. T. Misene, Georges Hugnet, Man Ray), 1934

Jacques-Emile Blanche. *Portrait of André Gide*, 1912. Musée des Beaux-Arts, Rouen

Man Ray. *André Breton*, c. 1932

republished to huge audiences during the 1920s.)

Although they professed indifference to literature as such, both Aragon and Breton contributed to the mutation of the modern novel. Aragon's *The Peasant of Paris*, published in 1926, proved that he had given himself completely to what he described as the "vice called Surrealism . . . the undisciplined and passionate use of the drug *image*." In this urban ramble, Aragon writes a first-person account of the innumerable marvels he encountered when he made himself available to everything that moved into view. A twentieth-century version of Baudelaire's *flâneur*, Aragon describes the Surrealists' haunts in the shabbier *quartiers* of Paris: their cafés, their entertainments in popular theaters, their gratuitous encounters, especially with women. Two years later, Breton published *Nadja*. In this novel the city is again the source and receptacle of hallucinatory images from Breton's psyche, and the everyday—signboards, public statuary, shop windows— takes on the heightened relief of dreams. Breton had succeeded in putting dream and reality on the same plane, an ideal he had established in his first manifesto.

With enormous energy the Surrealists sought out the talents that seemed congenial with their tenets. They were also alert to currents that contradicted their own, and mounted noisy offensives against such contradictions. Cocteau's theater drew their wrath. His much-quoted dictum from *Le Coq et l'Arlequin*, "Tact in audacity consists in knowing how far we may go too far," was anathema to the Surrealists. They threw their support to Antonin Artaud, whose "far" was always too far; who, as Aragon said in 1925, was "the man who has attacked the ocean." Artaud's extravagances did not prevent him from playing Tiresias in Cocteau's *Antigone* in 1922, with decor by Picasso and music by Honegger. But as time went on, his formulation for a new theater became diametrically opposed to Cocteau's.

Besides their interest in theater, the Surrealists kept an eye on the cinema, which they regarded as the optimal form for the expression of their aesthetic. Certainly the Surrealist spirit suffused the experimental films of Man Ray, an intimate member of the group. But it also crept into the work of René Clair, who produced *Entr'acte cinématographique (A Cinematographic*

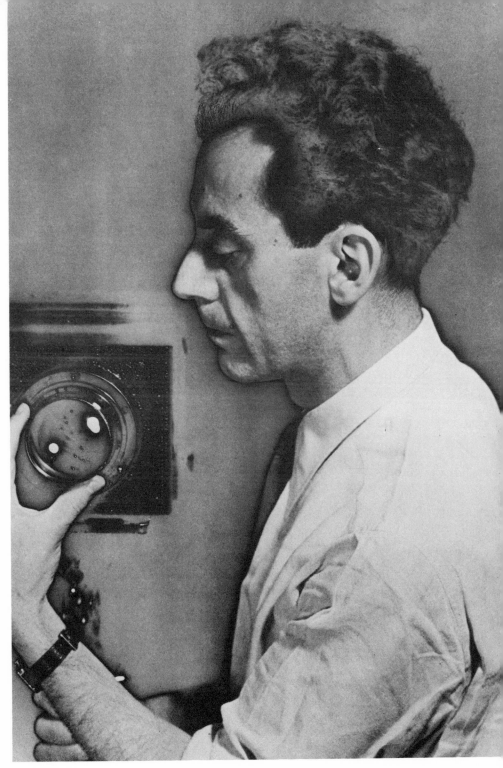

Man Ray. *Self-Portrait*, 1932

Intermission) in 1924 with an extravagance of juxtaposed images carefully matched in a score by Erik Satie. A year later Fernand Léger and Dudley Murphy produced the film *Ballet méchanique (Mechanical Ballet)*, which also owed something to the Surrealist excess, as did Georges Antheil's score that calls for saws, anvils, airplane propellers, and sixteen grand pianos. The Surrealist movie par excellence, *Un Chien andalou*, was presented in 1929. Breton was so smitten with it that he reproduced Buñuel's scenario in *La Révolution surréaliste*, and thenceforth often ran stills from Buñuel's films in the journal.

Many of Buñuel's preoccupations, above all his anticlericalism, paralleled those of the Surrealist band. But while Breton, Eluard, and other writers in the journal kept up a barrage against the reactionary politics of the French Catholic Church, a number of other intellectuals were finding their way back to the church. Even Cocteau, whose friend Max Jacob had converted long before (and regularly proselytized Cocteau), came perilously close to becoming a Catholic doctrinaire under the influence of Jacques and Raïssa Maritain. This resurgence of religion in certain intellectual circles sent the Surrealists into paroxysms of denunciation. But formal religion, as Julien Benda would point out in 1923 in his controversial book, *La Trahison des clercs (The Treason of the Intellectuals)*, was not the only snare in a world increasingly threatened politically. The same passions that had fomented religious persecutions, Benda maintained, were now activated by the "clerks"—intellectuals who no longer remained at a critical distance from social and political issues, who no longer put justice above all other considerations, but who, like Barrès, Maurras, and d'Annunzio, exercised the tendency to action, the thirst for immediate results, the exclusive preoccupation with the desired end, the scorn for argument, the excess, the hatred, the fixed ideas. . . .

The battle between the newly converted intellectuals and the atheistic Surrealists spilled over into the cafés and ateliers of the artists, and years later Giorgio de Chirico would recall, "In Paris there were two sorts of snobbery, especially among certain literati. One consisted of *making Catholics*, and so for certain literati, the so-called Catholic crisis was a classic event . . . The other . . . consisted of making atheists and anticlericals . . ."

The 1930s were ushered in by an appropriately disquieting event when the audience threw ink at the screen and rioted at the premiere of *L'Age d'or (The Golden Age)* by Buñuel and Dali. The film began with a chilling documentary on the habits of scorpions and then slid into the Surrealist mélange of images calculated to remind audiences of increasingly menacing social disorders. The success of Buñuel, who had originally planned a title taken from a phrase in the Communist Manifesto, "the icy waters of egoist calculation," was confirmed by the immediate outraged response of the very powers he was attacking. His radical Surrealism, true to the two vital sources of inspiration for the group during the late 1920s and 1930s—psychoanalysis and political radicalism—drew demands for censorship in *Le Figaro* in December 1930. The newspaper called the film "an essay in Bolshevism" whose Leninist propagandistic aim was to corrupt. It claimed that the film "publicly parades a collection of the most obscene, repellent, and witless episodes. Fatherland, family, and religion are all dragged through the mire." Buñuel's mastery of the language of images, put to the service of morality, was to be a lasting shock and a seminal lesson to future film-makers. Henry Miller regarded the film as the most important ever made. He called Buñuel "the man who flings dynamite."

At the same time that Buñuel had received a commission from the Vicomte de Noailles to help pay for *L'Age d'or*, Jean Cocteau had also been commissioned by Noailles to make a film. He embarked on his cinematic apprenticeship with *Le Sang d'un poète (The Blood of a Poet)*. Although the film strictly adhered to Cocteau's conviction that there were no politics in art, his film generated considerable uneasiness. His very technique—the juxtaposition of concrete images to produce a sense of unreality akin to the process of dreaming—was calculated to disturb. Cocteau claimed that this was an anti-Surrealist film, and one devoid of symbolism. He called it "a realistic documentary of unreal events." Yet some of the Surrealists' favorite images appeared: the collapsing factory chimneys that open and close the film recall de Chirico, the early shots of hands echo Breton's

Amedeo Modigliani. *Jean Cocteau*, 1917. The Henry and Rose Pearlman Foundation

fascination with hands and gloves in *Nadja*, the peepshows at the doorways in the fantastic hotel are motifs explored in Surrealist literature, and the deployment of such objects as guns and fireplaces and mirrors recall Magritte's paintings, which were reproduced frequently in Surrealist publications during the late 1920s.

The burgeoning preoccupation with objects manifested in Surrealist art suggested a world in which man, for all his psychological complexity, was still not master. During the early 1930s, Alberto Giacometti offered some startling sculptures in which the object is seen as a cruel menace to the equanimity of man. *The Captured Hand* of 1932, for instance, entices the spectator to turn a crank that will guillotine the hand. Giacometti's gloomy forebodings were further expressed in a sculpture of the same year, *Woman with Her Throat Cut*. The all-but-vanishing, wraithlike figures in Giacometti's sculpture after 1935 relate in their isolation to Sartre's characterization of Roquetin in *La Nausée (Nausea)* (published in 1938) as a man who, having divested himself of all received ideas or values, found himself existing alone, but in the world that is incontrovertibly there. At the same time, Picasso was elaborating his reflection on the *corrida*, and toward the mid-1930s produced a series of drawings and a print on the theme of the Minotauromachy that was a portent of the calamity he was to commemorate in the great 1937 mural, *Guernica*. When in 1935 Giacometti broke with the Surrealists and set out to explore the human visage, he reflected the extreme emotional disarray of the times; the anxiety, the violence, the crushing events that were later to be interpreted by his friend Jean-Paul Sartre in his writings on Existentialism.

There were many signs that the reevaluation of values called for at the turn of the century had come to a desperate pass. Violent and tragic imagery crested during the late 1920s—a symptom of the age that Antonin Artaud boldly explored when he published his manifesto for a "Theater of Cruelty" in the *Nouvelle Revue Française* in 1932. It began, "We cannot go on prostituting the idea of the theater, which is valid only when there is a magical and agonizing relationship with reality and with danger . . ."

Artaud's diction in much of his writing during the early 1930s took on an exalted, sometimes hysterical tone. One of his favorite metaphors was that of fire, which would sweep spectators into its roaring heart and awaken them to the great spiritual dangers he sensed in the world. Once, after a lecture at the Sorbonne in 1933 in which he was mercilessly heckled, he walked out with Anaïs Nin, sadly reflecting that "They always want to hear *about* . . . and I want to give them the experience itself so that they will be terrified and awaken."

The animus against Naturalism implicit in Artaud's Theater of Cruelty smoldered in another striking event of 1932: the publication of Louis-Ferdinand Céline's novel, *Voyage au bout de la nuit (Journey to the End of the Night)*. The force of Céline's hatred for the devastated postwar world smote French readers with the terror of recognition. Céline's uninhibited language, his bitterness, his vernacular style, his flights into hideous fantasies, gave shape to a state of mind, an exasperation that was widely shared. A few years later, when he embarked on the savage, nihilistic campaign that eventually brought him to the courtroom to face charges of treason, Gide, writing in the April 1938 issue of *Nouvelle Revue Française*, summed him up as a man who excels in invective: "It is not reality that Céline paints; it is the hallucination that reality provokes."

The enormity of the realities confronting Europe seemed to provoke cruel hallucinations in many quarters. Not only did many writers sense the coming war on the horizon, they also had to recognize that political structures in France itself were no longer tenable. By 1933 there were a million and a half unemployed. Economic and political turbulence had become a daily affair. After the riots of 1934 and the ominous march of some forty thousand uniformed members of the *Croix de Feu* (many of them Nazi sympathizers) in 1935, artists and writers seemed convinced of at least one thing: they would have to enter the fray. They had already told themselves that the fight against fascism was their first duty in the famous First International Congress of Writers for the Defense of Culture held in June 1935, presided over by André Gide, and animated by such militants as Louis Aragon, Henri Barbusse, and André Malraux.

While the Congress called upon writers of the Left from all over the world, there is some question, as Roger Shattuck sees it, as to whether it could ever have constituted a nexus of real forces, and what its tangible results could have been. However, Shattuck wrote, "Of this much I feel sure; the thirties worried their way through a prolonged economic and political crisis that threw intellectuals and artists into a state of increasing tension. The Congress is a surprisingly clear window on that decade." A year later, France astonishingly enough elected a man of letters, a refined, intelligent Socialist, Léon Blum, to preside over the short-lived Popular Front. Blum's failure, brought about partly by his indecision concerning the Spanish Civil War, was perceived by many intellectuals as the final stage in the total disintegration of France. Artists and writers who had succumbed for a time to the notion that their own engagement in the political process could make a difference crept back into isolation, feeling once again alienated, as they had felt for more than a century.

For the French avant-garde, the second World War was in many respects grimmer than the first. In occupied Paris, life was filled with privation and fear. Friendships were sundered over the issue of participation or neutrality. A number of young aspirants to the vanguard joined the Resistance. Older figures, including Cocteau, maintained an uncomfortable, ambivalent existence, sometimes coming into direct social contact with their Nazi conquerors. Cocteau's position was, as always, apolitical, and his erstwhile colleagues did not seem to resent it. When his old friend Max Jacob was finally wrenched from his ecclesiastical retreat by the Nazis, his final appeal for help went out to Cocteau, who immediately attempted to have Otto Abetz rescind the deportation order, without success.

Jacob's letter was surely one of the great sorrows of Cocteau's wartime years:

Dear Jean,
 I am writing to you in a train with the indulgence of the police who surround us.
 We will soon be at Drancy.
 That is all I have to say.

Sacha when they spoke to him of my sister said, "If it were he, I could do something."

Well, it's me.

Jacob, along with the Surrealist poet Robert Desnos and countless others, died in the camps. The frightful absurdity of their deaths was not lost on the new generation of intellectuals, among them Sartre and Camus, whose writings insistently confronted the issue of evil made so urgent during the war.

These participants in the Resistance felt a kinship with the older members of the avant-garde, and gathered from time to time during the war. One of the often-recalled highlights of that gray time was the performance of Picasso's absurdist farce in the spirit of *Ubu Roi, Le Désir attrapé par la queue (Desire Caught by the Tail)* in March 1944. Held in the home of the Surrealist poet and anthropologist Michel Leiris, the play was directed by Camus, with Raymond Queneau, Sartre, Dora Maar, Simone de Beauvoir, and Georges Hugnet among those taking part. Ridiculous as the plot and the characters are, the play managed through hilarity to conjure up the authentic sufferings brought on by the war, a strategy that was later to be brought to its highest pitch by the postwar dramatist, Eugene Ionesco.

It was during the war that Cocteau "discovered" another of the dramatists who was to make his indelible mark in the immediate postwar period. Jean Genet was still in prison when Cocteau read his poetry and declared him a great writer. When Genet came to trial, Cocteau defended him and begged the court to pardon him. After the war, Genet presented his first incendiary play, *The Maids*—a wrathful vision of degradation, which, in its need to revolt and shock, owed a large debt to Artaud. Genet brought the ignoble passions of jealousy, hatred, and murderousness into a ritual context that set Paris quivering. This "event," and the performance a year later of *Deathwatch*, were comparable, in their *succès de scandale*, to Buñuel's time-bomb films. While Cocteau invested great energy in promoting Genet, who also found vigorous supporters among the Existentialists, led by Sartre, he himself was turning toward another, more benign vision. In 1944 the photographer Brassaï talked with him at Picasso's studio. Cocteau said, "If poets were to take over the

Jean Cocteau
par
Francis Picabia
1921

Francis Picabia. *Jean Cocteau*, 1921. Musée National d'Art Moderne, Paris

cinema, it could become the royal highway of poetry." By August 1945 Cocteau was at work on the royal highway, shooting *La Belle et la bête (Beauty and the Beast)*, a film that brought to its height Cocteau's ability to transform the cinema.

The tender poetry of Cocteau's film was well received, but youth in the postwar years was seeking more trenchant messages. When Artaud gave his last performance—an appearance at the Théâtre du Vieux-Colombier on January 13, 1947—the hall was thronged with young people, who joined Breton, Barrault, Paulhan, Adamov, and Camus. Gide reported that "Of his material existence, nothing remained except what was expressive . . . reason beat a retreat—not only his but that of the whole assembly, all of us spectators of this atrocious drama reduced to the role of malevolent supernumeraries, mere nobodies . . ."

Reason beat a retreat; in theater, the Theater of the Absurd burgeoned, drawing upon the traditions of both Artaud and Jarry. In philosophy, the Existentialists swept throughout the Western world with their resurrection of the great thunderers against unexamined reason, Kierkegaard, Nietzsche, and Dostoevski. In painting and sculpture, artists rushed to denounce the reasonable geometries of the prewar period, taking the Surrealist stance that the unconscious was the richest source of artistic truth. The "informal" painters soon found themselves matched by the American Abstract Expressionists, who had also eschewed the more rationalist modes of Cubism in favor of an expression of the inner life through the association of images. The boulevard bookstores during the 1950s were well stocked with texts that fed rebellious instincts, including many on mysticism, alchemy, and the nostrums of such cult figures as Gurdjieff.

"Intellectual despair winds up neither in apathy nor in the dream, but in violence," said Georges Bataille, defining the peculiarities of moral despair in 1929. The postwar generation of the second World War in France was still in its grip. Throughout the years leading up to the revolt of 1968, there was a steady hum of violent dissent in French intellectual life, from Camus's publication of *Man in Revolt* in 1951 to Sartre's advocacy of civil disobedience during the war in Algeria. Artists and writers veered from the subjective emotionalism of the informal to the deliberately cold and dehumanizing tone of the *nouveau roman*. In each case, the extreme belied a violent impatience and a fundamental pessimism. As in all truculent epochs, there was a simultaneous feeling of continuity and discontinuity, a strong sense that the Western World had, in Ubu Roi's words, destroyed even the ruins. And there was also a sense that nonetheless, the work of creative minds would go on—as it always had.

Man Ray. *Portrait of Cocteau,* 1922

Jean Cocteau and the Image d'Epinal

An Essay on Realism and Naiveté*

Kenneth E. Silver

IF HE WAS NOT ITS INVENTOR, Jean Cocteau was nonetheless the great popularizer of an aesthetic of innocence—a love of the everyday and the naive—that he himself first refined before transmitting to twentieth-century audiences. Cocteau's discussion of Nijinska's choreography for *Les Biches (The Does)*—the Ballets Russes production of 1924, with music by Francis Poulenc and sets and costumes by Marie Laurencin—could well stand as the credo for his aesthetic. "Her brother's blood runs in her veins," he wrote of Nijinsky's sister,

> . . . a blood with wings. She does not try to discover what there is at the back of Poulenc or Laurencin. She is guided by intuition. Without the slightest calculation, and by simply obeying the rhythm, and the exigencies of the frame she has to fill, she is about to create a masterpiece: the *Fêtes Galantes* of her time.
>
> To have thought about *Fêtes Galantes*, to have thought about the hidden audacities which specialists discover in a Watteau tree . . . to have thought about art, in short to have thought at all, would have meant losing the game.[1]

*The title of this essay is intended as an homage by the author to Meyer Schapiro's essay of 1941, *Courbet and Popular Imagery (An Essay on Realism and Naiveté)*.

Needless to say, Cocteau himself thought a great deal about a great many things: about rococo picnics, about the bravura brushwork of Watteau, and about art in general. But what he admires most is the very opposite of this ratiocination—the untutored, intuitively audacious artist like Nijinska, who wins the game by virtue of her purity. Of course, this search for savage nobility is a well-established aspect of Cocteau's aesthetic and of his romantic inclinations (which were usually indistinguishable): his discovery of the boy poet Raymond Radiguet was the fulfillment of a poetic idea—*le naif au corps*. Largely unrecognized, however, is the visual component of Jean Cocteau's "aesthetic of innocence," which exerted considerable influence on the art of the Parisian avant-garde. I would like to discuss here Cocteau's visual tastes, as manifested both verbally and in visual art in the decade of his first maturity, between the time of the outbreak of the Great War and the mid-1920s. I will focus especially on the major public events, the theater productions, with which Cocteau was involved during these years.

It is worth recalling that, before World War I, Cocteau had been a minor though not insignificant member of the circle around Diaghilev's Ballets Russes. In 1911 he designed two well-known if aesthetically unremarkable posters for the Monte Carlo premiere of Fokine's *Spectre de la Rose (Specter of the Rose)*: a pair of lithographic portraits of Nijinsky as the roseate spirit and Karsavina as the swooning Young Girl; then, in 1912, along with Frédéric de Madrazo, he wrote the scenario for the unsuccessful Ballets Russes production of *Le Dieu bleu (The Blue God)*. Set to the music of Reynaldo Hahn, with sumptuous decor and costumes by Léon Bakst, and danced by Nijinsky and Karsavina, it was an "oriental" ballet of the kind for which the troupe was beloved by the Parisian Right Bank. The libretto concerned a devout young man who wanders into a miraculous clime, "where crowds of people perform ritual dances dressed in the saffron robe of those who serve the Lotus." Nijinsky portrayed the Blue God, a none-too-subtle spectral transformation of his celebrated earlier role. Although *Le Dieu bleu* was soon dropped from the repertory, it is important in establishing

Léon Bakst. Costume design for *Le Dieu bleu*, 1912. Musée National **>** d'Art Moderne, Paris

Cocteau's involvement with the voluptuous, exotic aesthetic of the Ballets Russes, because it was in part against this that the poet reacted so abruptly and emphatically after August 1914.

Indeed, it wasn't even Cocteau's own idea to turn against the prewar aesthetic of the Russian Ballet. For shortly after the outbreak of war, this exotic art, which had been so popular with the Parisian *gratin*, the fashionable society, was stigmatized as *boche*—decadent, unpatriotic, "cosmopolitan," dangerous, and Germanic. The extreme right-wing critic, Léon Daudet, son of Alphonse (and brother of Lucien, one of Cocteau's good friends), had this to say in *Hors du Joug Allemand (Outside the German Yoke)*, a celebrated anti-German tract of 1915: "After German Hellenism, we had German Orientalism, this screeching modernism of the aesthetic, of which the discontent are so proud . . . Nonetheless, in these gaudy monstrosities, one can still make out aspirations of German imperialism, the training of her sights on Baghdad and elsewhere . . . these theatrical 'Turkish-isms' have a political significance." In 1915 the couturier Paul Poiret was called a German collaborator in the pages of a popular magazine, *La Renaissance*, and accused of having foisted oriental culottes and turbans, inspired by the Ballets Russes, on the innocent women of Paris. Poiret's wartime travails are an absurd if unfortunately true example of cultural xenophobia, one that concluded, however, two years after the initial slander, with the designer's exoneration. Many well-known Parisian figures came to Poiret's defense, including Max Jacob, André Dunoyer de Segonzac, Jacques-Emile Blanche, and Raoul Dufy (the opposition was made up mostly of bureaucrats). Significantly, Jean Cocteau was not among Poiret's supporters, despite the fact that he had been an intimate of the designer before the war. He claimed in a letter published in the last issue of the magazine that "it would be necessary to establish nuances which prohibit me from signing *en bloc*," that is, from signing a petition in Poiret's support. But Cocteau seems never to have had a strongly developed moral sense—perhaps because his personal struggles as a homosexual were too overwhelming, or perhaps from simple selfishness. Be that as it may, it is in any case not

Jean Cocteau. *"Dante Avec Nous,"* cover of *Le Mot,* June 15,1915

surprising that Cocteau was wary of appearing to endorse Poiret's "decadent" prewar tastes during wartime, for he was busily trying to extricate himself from the same stigma.

By the time that he declined to speak in support of Paul Poiret, in late 1917, Cocteau had already traversed an enormous distance in artistic sensibility. Together with the designer Paul Iribe, he had founded and edited the little wartime magazine *Le Mot*, which first appeared November 1914, less than four months after the beginning of war. The magazine's tone was strongly nationalistic and anti-German, although its jingoism was more light-hearted and stylish than that of the more conventional magazines. Nonetheless, it represented a *volte-face* for a figure like Cocteau, who had been at the very center of cosmopolitan Paris only a few months previous. "The *métèque* [i.e., foreigner] cannot love our journal," he wrote in issue no. 7, January 1915, and this was supported by all kinds of visual slurs against the enemy in the form of line drawings that Cocteau drew under the name of "Jim." It was also in *Le Mot* that the poet offered his confreres in the Parisian avant-garde a formula for finessing their way through the stormy waters of wartime public opinion: "Between TASTE and VULGARITY, both unpleasant, there remains an elan and a measure: THE TACT OF UNDERSTANDING HOW FAR TO GO TOO FAR. *Le Mot* hopes you will follow it on this path of France."

But exactly what was the high road of French culture that Cocteau was recommending, now that he had dissociated himself from Ballets Russes exoticism? Apart from the prewar tastes he maintained and wrote about in *Le Mot*—for the poetry of Anna de Noailles and Valéry-Larbaud, for Stravinsky's music and Bonnard's painting—he had moved away from Right Bank Orientalism toward Left Bank bohemianism. Among *Le Mot*'s favorite painters were the emphatically Cubist Albert Gleizes and the marginally Cubist Roger de la Fresnaye. Still, Cocteau did not have much that was favorable to say about Cubism as a movement. In June 1915, he wrote: "Cubism was convenient for a large public . . . Cubism was convenient and a little simple, as Impressionism was, in its time," but went on: "Let's hope that the postwar will bring the death of the 'ism,'" and then concluded: "Let's be on guard against German-Ism."

Of course, after Cocteau's famous meeting only a few months later with Pablo Picasso—a rendezvous that he felt was "written in the stars"—his pronouncements on Cubism were very different indeed. Now, for instance, he could say, "Don't fool yourself . . . Cubism was a classicism after the romanticism of the Fauves,"[2] or more typically, he would set Impressionism up as the straw man to be knocked down by Cubism (we must remember that the Impressionist aesthetic was still powerful, even in 1915, although perhaps more as a symbol than a visual model; in effect, it was the father figure of avant-garde revolt). In a little-known brochure that he wrote in 1918, *Dans le Ciel de la patrie (In the Sky of the Fatherland)*, a patriotic advertisement for the SPAD aircraft company, Cocteau wrote, irrelevant to either aircraft or patriotism: "The Impressionist painter looked at nature through eyes squinting at the sun; today Cubism rediscovers that austere discipline of the great epochs, renounces charming games, and the universe again becomes the pretext for a new architecture of the sensibility;"[3] in 1917 he copied down something that Picasso had said to him in Rome: "Work with three colors: too many colors make Impressionism."[4]

When it came to discussing music, the word Impressionism—used to describe the music of Debussy—had an even more important role to play. *Le Coq et l'Arlequin (The Cock and the Harlequin)* of 1918, a small book of musical theory (perhaps one might better call it, as Cocteau himself did, *"notes autour de la musique")* (notes around music), is frankly nationalistic; what he wanted was a "French music for France," which meant a renunciation of the prevailing "Germanic-Slavo musical labyrinth." This led Cocteau to such statements as: "Impressionism was a rebound off of Wagner," and "Debussy transposes Claude Monet into Russian," while "Satie remains intact . . . Satie speaks of Ingres." Here, late in the war, he distinguishes two spheres of artistic sensibility: a prewar aesthetic of Romanticism, Impressionism, vagueness, complication, and exotic tastes, and a post-1914 return to clarity, light, and Latin simplicity—the appropriate style for French art. "The Latin game is played without pushing on the pedals," he wrote. "Romanticism pushed on the pedals; pedal Wagner; Debussy pedal." When, a few years later, Cocteau said that "Picasso . . . is conscious of the inferiority of arabesques and spots, which he leaves to mere decorators," he had found a slightly cryptic but economical formula for unburdening Picasso of the Orientalist and Impressionist aesthetics.

Yet if Cocteau had fully divested himself of arabesques and spots, there is no meaningful sense in which he became a Cubist either. Although it is true that after 1917 he was regularly invoking the term, Cubism for Cocteau was a rhetorical device, a shorthand way of expressing the values of the Left Bank, of modernism and artistic experimentation; he liked the sound of it, but he never seems to have really liked its looks. Neither in his famous line drawings (which were adaptations of Picasso's Ingres-style draftsmanship) nor in *Le Boeuf sur le toit (The Ox on the Roof)* of 1920 and *Les Mariés de la Tour Eiffel (The Wedding on the Eiffel Tower)* of 1921, the two theatrical productions that succeeded *Parade*, do we find even a trace of Cubism. But let us take another look at *Parade*, Cocteau's famous collaboration with Picasso in 1917.

It is worthwhile to recall Cocteau's scenario, which can be told in the poet's own words.

Parade. Realist ballet.
The decor represents the houses of Paris on a Sunday. *Théâtre forain* [traveling theatre]. Three music hall numbers serve as the Parade.
Chinese prestidigitator.
Acrobats.
Little American girl.

Three managers organize the publicity. They communicate in their extraordinary language that the crowd should join the parade to see the show inside and grossly try to make it [the crowd] understand this.
No one enters.
After the last act of the parade, the exhausted managers collapse on each other.

The Chinese, the acrobats and the little girl leave the empty theater. Seeing the supreme effort and the failure of the managers, they in turn try to explain that the show takes place inside.

The point of the story is clear enough: it is a parable of the travails of the avant-garde, whereby the public is not interested in making the kind of effort necessary to appreciate new (and true) art. The production's Cubist aspects are, of course, quite famous: Picasso designed a somewhat fragmented cityscape and skewed proscenium arch for the setting, as well as two Cubist constructions for the Managers, one "in evening dress" and one "from New York." In addition, Cocteau's insertion of nonmusical sounds into Satie's score has been taken as an example of Cubism, although it is probably less confusing to use the word "collage" for this (a term not necessarily synonymous with Cubism).

But at least as important as the Cubist qualities of the ballet are the non-Cubist, and largely traditional, aspects of *Parade*, not only Picasso's designs for the costumes of the Chinese Magician, the Acrobats, and the Little American Girl, but also the great painted overture curtain, which was the first thing that the audience at the Châtelet saw when the house curtain went up on the afternoon of May 18, 1917. Indeed, although there have been attempts to provide "Cubist" interpretations of the depiction, namely, Richard Axsom's extensive analysis of the overture curtain as a Cubist work, it was intended to be, and to appear, just as traditional as it is in fact. Based on an early nineteenth-century Neapolitan gouache by Achille Vianelli,[5] it depicts two groups. At the right, around a table, is gathered a theatrical troupe that includes two Harlequins, two young women of the "pretty peasant" type, an Italian sailor, a Spanish guitarist, a blackamoor, and a faithful dog at their feet. In the group at the left is a small circus act that is entertaining the group at the right, including a winged bareback rider atop a mare got up as Pegasus, a suckling foal, and a monkey climbing a ladder. Not surprisingly in the midst of war, this scene of sublimely Latin sentiment was meant as a demonstration of the virtues of the Mediterranean, "classical" way of life—a life that France, along with her ally, Italy, considered to be in danger of imminent extinction by the barbarian German hordes. It is hardly accidental that Picasso's palette is predominantly blue, white, and red, the colors of the French *tricolore*, or that a fourth predominant

Pablo Picasso. Costume for the Manager, *Parade*, 1917

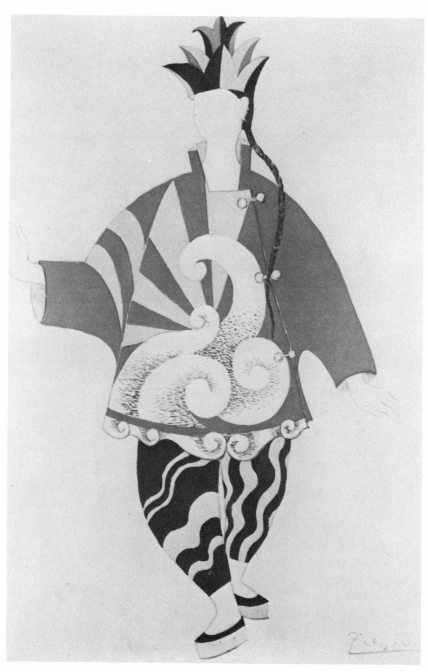

Pablo Picasso. *Chinese Magician*, costume for *Parade*, 1917. Private collection, Paris

color is green, providing an alternate, Italianate *tricolore*. In an article that was published in *L'Excelsior* the same day as *Parade*'s premiere, Cocteau, by way of justifying the production, wrote, "Our wish is that the public may consider *Parade* as a work that conceals poetry beneath the coarse outer skin of *guignol* . . . Laughter is natural to Frenchmen . . . Laughter is too Latin a weapon to be neglected."

Indeed, to ignore the production's willed classical and traditional elements and refer to it as a Cubist ballet (Cocteau, of course, made a point of calling it a "realist" ballet) is both to misunderstand *Parade*'s aesthetic and also to imply that it was exclusively or primarily Picasso's. What makes *Parade* what it is, for better or worse, is the juxtaposition of illusionistic and abstract elements, not the absorbing of the former into the latter. Or it might be put another way: *Parade* resulted from the meeting of two sensibilities, Cocteau's and Picasso's, the former providing the traditional elements, the latter the abstract ones. In fact, Cocteau later discussed *Parade* in almost those terms:

> I understood that there existed in Paris an artistic Right and an artistic Left, which were ignorant or disdainful of each other for no valid reasons and which it was perfectly possible to bring together. It was a question of converting Diaghilev to modern painting and converting the modern painters, especially Picasso, to the sumptuous, decorative aesthetic of the ballet; of coaxing the Cubists out of their isolation, persuading them to abandon their hermetic Montmartre folklore . . . the discovery of a middle-of-the-road solution attuned to the taste for luxury and pleasure, of the revived cult of French "clarity" . . . such was the history of *Parade*.[6]

But of course, Cocteau's contribution to *Parade* was more personal, and more specific, than the word "traditional" can convey. For the conventions on which the ballet depends for its meaning are those of the *arts populaires—guignol, commedia dell'arte,* circus, *saltimbanques*, music hall—a taste for which, by 1917, had an impressive pedigree in French painting, going back at least as far as Watteau. In *Parade*, though, the character who embodies the spirit of innocent enthusiasm and popular tastes is of the New World: the Little American Girl, whose *vita activa* assumes an especially modern, uncontemplative form. Here, in part, is how Cocteau described the Little American Girl to Erik

Satie: "The Titanic—'Nearer My God to Thee'—elevators . . . The New York Herald . . . Walt Whitman—the silence of stampedes—cowboys with leather and goatskin chaps . . . the Sioux . . . Beautiful Madame Astor . . . projectors—arc-lamps—gramophones—typewriters—the Eiffel Tower—the Brooklyn Bridge . . . Charlie Chaplin—Christopher Columbus . . . the isle of Mauritius—*Paul et Virginie.*" Where he begins and ends his description is significant: he starts with the sinking of the Titanic and finishes with Paul and Virginia on their tropical island. In Cocteau's mind, the Little American Girl will always end up on her feet; she is the survivor who, thanks to her innocence and her superb instincts, can withstand the assaults of the modern world. She is the modern version of those darlings of French children's literature, Paul and Virginia, who in Bernardin de Saint-Pierre's novel survive a shipwreck to find themselves stranded in a new Eden. For Cocteau, popular culture is reminiscent of childhood; High Art is the work of adults.

But we can be still more precise in describing Cocteau's aesthetic of innocence, because there is a major visual source for his sensibility, crucial to his artistic development during and after World War I and for his sensibility in general, the *image d'Epinal* —the crude, folkloric, brightly colored broadsides (first woodcut, then after 1850 lithographic), produced since the sixteenth century in Epinal, a town in Lorraine in eastern France. From early on, the artifacts of popular culture had fired the poet's imagination. After reading Rimbaud's *Illuminations,* Cocteau said that he suddenly "understood everything," and Frederick Brown has pointed out that later Cocteau paraphrased a famous passage from *Une Saison en enfer (A Season in Hell)* in which the Symbolist poet declared his youthful passion for "idiotic paintings, decorative panels, circus backdrops, shop signs, popular prints, unfashionable literature, Church Latin, erotic prose misspelled, or ancestors' novels, fairy tales, little children's books, old operas, silly refrains, naive songs."[7]

It wasn't until *Le Mot,* however, that Cocteau had the opportunity—an ideal one—to demonstrate his ever-increasing interest in and taste for the naive and *populaire.* The magazine was mainly illustrated with his own patriotic, pro-Allied, anti-German cartoons and sketches, but it also featured other work, including new wartime versions of the old *images d'Epinal*. Raoul Dufy's 1915 print, *La Fin de la grande guerre (The End of the Great War)*, appeared in issue no. 13. Here, to the tune of the folk-song "The Wandering Jew"—itself a popular subject of nine-teenth-century popular prints—the *coq Gaulois*, Chantecleer, sings a hymn to victory; the German eagle is crushed beneath his claw and he is surrounded by vignettes drawn from the national mythology—pictures of Marshal Joffre, Jeanne d'Arc, and the cathedral of Reims in flames. (The bombing of Reims by the Germans in the fall of 1914, early in the war, remained a prime symbol of German barbarism thereafter.) Of another of Dufy's timely *images d'Epinal*, published in issue no. 10, Cocteau told his readers approvingly, "*Voilà de l'excellente tradition d'Epinal tricolore . . .*" Whether he was aware of it or not, there were good reasons for featuring these new-fangled wartime versions of the old-fashioned images in *Le Mot*, the same reasons that, as critic Clément Janin noted in the *Gazette des Beaux-Arts* in 1917, were "Still another effect of the war: the renaissance of the *image d'Epinal!*" Not only was the *image d'Epinal*, with its simple format and equally simple delineation, easy to imitate and to produce, but just as in the past, it was an art form designed to appeal to a large audience—a truly popular art. Moreover, it was indisputably French and effective at arousing public sentiment in a war that was intended as *revanche* for the humiliation of 1870—the town of Epinal was in the captured province of Lorraine, which France hoped to retrieve.

Equally important in explaining the wartime popularity of *image d'Epinal*, as Janin also pointed out, was its essentially didactic character. Comparing the new crop of wartime Epinal images to photographs, which served as documents, the critic said, "Obviously, the image *[d'Epinal]* provides something else. It is less documentary than allegorical. The portrait, notably, aspires to nothing other than a purely moral truth; it responds to the idea that the public has of a person, rather than to his reality. The battles that they show are those of the imagination, but they have a sense of action, a feel for the character of the ensemble, that the photographic document does not, because

Raoul Dufy. *La Fin de la grande guerre*, 1915. Reproduced in *Le Mot*,
no. 13, March 6, 1915

the mind has conceived this ensemble."[8] Along with the image's
claim to a certain kind of Frenchness, and aside from its various
patriotic, naive, and artistic associations, Cocteau was also
attracted to the popular print for its moralizing function. Indeed,
although we have already said that after 1914 Cocteau was
neither Impressionist nor Orientalist nor Cubist, we must also
say that he was not a realist either—certainly not in Courbet's
sense of the term, nor by an empiricist's definition. He called
Parade "realist" to distinguish it from Cubism, and also to
make the point that his ballet referred to something ordinary
rather than to an arcane, "grown-up" aesthetic. Cocteau's artistic realism, such as it was, did, however, offer two kinds of

truths: his audience would witness the true story of the artist's attempt to capture the public's attention, and it would be told with all the truth of myth—the struggle of the artist would be portrayed as an eternal struggle for recognition. *Parade* was a parable drawn from the reality of daily Parisian life.

It was this kind of realism that Cocteau subsequently exploited in *Le Boeuf sur le toit* and in *Les Mariés de la Tour Eiffel*—a realism of convention, of types, stereotypes, and archetypes. He had no interest whatsoever in individuals, in the particularities of character (perhaps in part because his classical sense dictated that the public medium of theater demanded generalization of character). In all three productions, in his libretti and in the designs he commissioned to realize his stories, Cocteau presents a conventionalized humanity much as it appears in the *images d'Epinal*. In *Parade* there are no proper names, only descriptions: the Chinese Magician, the Little American Girl, the Acrobats, the Managers; in *Le Boeuf sur le toit*, again no names, but types: the Woman in a Low-Cut Dress, the Red-Headed Woman, the Barman, the Policeman, the Negro Boxer; and again, in *Les Mariés*, an archetypal humanity: "the Bride, sweet as a lamb," "the Father-in-Law, rich as Croesus," "the Groom, pretty as a heart," "the Mother-in-Law, phoney as a slug," and other characters, such as the Director of the Eiffel Tower and the Bathing Beauty from Trouville.

For Cocteau, this use of stereotypes was an act both of restoration and of transubstantiation—on the one hand he would give meaning back to forms that had fallen into desuetude, on the other he would elevate the quotidian by means of his special powers. Of *Les Mariés de la Tour Eiffel*, he said: "I'm the one who rejuvenates the commonplace, places it, presents it from a special angle so that it becomes young again. A generation of obscurities, of tired-out realisms, is not easily disregarded. I know that my text may appear too simple, too clearly written, like children's alphabets. But really, aren't we still in school? Aren't we still deciphering the primary symbols?"

The set for *Les Mariés*, which takes place on one of the tiers of the Eiffel Tower, was designed for Cocteau by his friend Irène Lagut, an amateur artist who was able to provide just the right

Guy-Pierre Fauconnet, Raoul Dufy. Costumes and masks for *"La dame décolletée"* and *"Le barman"* from *Le Boeuf sur le toit*, 1920
Darius Milhaud Archive

touch of genuine naiveté; Jean Hugo, another close friend, created the costumes and masks, which combined, as Cocteau said, "an atavism of the real and the monstrous."[9] Both sets and costumes, undoubtedly at the author's instigation, were inspired by the work of Paris's most famous Sunday painter, the Douanier Rousseau, an untrained artist of astonishing powers (who was forever cribbing not only figures but whole compositions from magazines, postcards, encyclopedia pages, advertisements, bad academic art, and even from *images d'Epinal*). But once Cocteau has alerted us to the fact that he was thinking of children's alphabets, of tired-out realisms and commonplaces, we recognize the direct influence that the *images d'Epinal* exerted. Among the most famous genres of images produced at Epinal was the *"Cris de Paris,"* the centuries-old visual lexicon of the street vendors whose "cries" were usually arranged in alphabets, as in the *"alphabet grotesque."* Especially good for children's reading lessons, a Parisian "cry" was found for each letter of the alphabet—for example, "A" for *Allumettes chimiques*, "B" for

Balais! Balais!, "C" for *Chapeaux à vendre!*, and so forth. In fact, for *Les Mariés de la Tour Eiffel* Cocteau himself provided the "cries" for his characters, as each of their qualities was announced through one of two giant "phonographs" situated at the left and right of the stage; the dancers—the ballet was performed by Rolf de Maré's Ballets Suédois—moved to choreography by Cocteau and Jean Börlin, presumably in the stiff, doll-like gestures suggested by the popular prints. Cocteau said that he had used "all the popular Parisian resources" in order to entertain his Parisian audience.

The *image d'Epinal* versions of the *"Cris de Paris"* were even more important, although purely as a visual source, for the ballet *Le Boeuf sur le toit*, of the previous year. Cocteau had asked Darius Milhaud to compose music based on folk themes,

Jean Hugo. Costume sketches for *Les Mariés de la Tour Eiffel* (The Bridegroom

to accompany his little story (subtitled the *Nothing-Happens Bar*) of a "typical" American speakeasy during Prohibition. Guy-Pierre Fauconnet originally designed the costumes and masks, but he unfortunately died in the middle of preparations. Raoul Dufy—himself a *dévoté*, as we know, of the *image d'Epinal*—agreed to take over the work. Whether it was his idea, or Fauconnet's, or even more likely, Cocteau's, the resulting characters are quotations from the *images d'Epinal*—the enormous heads on tiny bodies almost certainly derive from a stylization that was standard for the "*Cris de Paris*," where the head was emphasized as the embodiment of the peddler's cry. Cocteau did not have to remind his audience that they had seen figures like these before; they were mostly Parisians who had grown up picturing the world through the same visual conventions that

Bride, Mother-in-law, and Father-in-law), 1921. Musée de la Danse, Stockholm

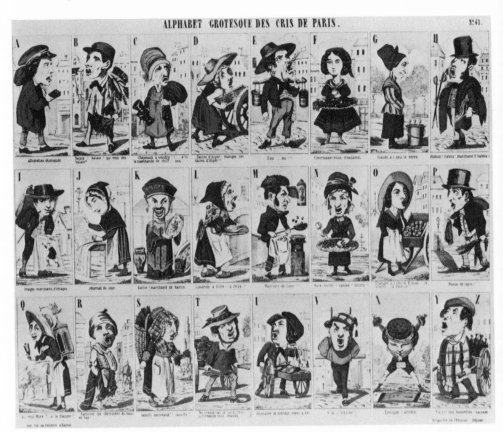

Anonymous. *Alphabet Grotesque des Cris de Paris*, 1858
Collection Bibliotheque National, Paris

had so impressed themselves upon the poet.

In fact, the *images d'Epinal* were also, surely, the major inspiration for the story and the visual aesthetic of *Parade*, which is nothing other than a magically transformed page of the "*Cris de Paris*," wherein the Parisian vendors have become artists, critics, and dealers trying desperately to catch the public's attention. In Cocteau's notes for *Parade* it is the word "*crier*"—not *houer*, *hurler*, or *pousser*—that recurs, as in "*Cris des trois managers*," and "*Parade/Cris/crier/cris*."[10] Luckily, owing to Picasso's early sketches for the Managers, we can trace the evolution of the idea of using the "*Cris de Paris*" as it must have first been suggested to the artist by Cocteau. We can see how closely the early, partially Cubist idea for the Manager is modeled on the Parisian street vendors of the "*Cris*," many of whom were famous for carrying their wares on their backs—note especially the letter "I" in our example, who is the "*marchand d'images*" (in fact, he is the merchant of *images d'Epinals*!), a bit of self-advertising that the Pellerin printers included in this and other similar alphabets; note also the drink vendor at the letter "Q," the salsify peddler at "S," and especially the *Vitrier*, who always carried his panes of glass on his back like so many free-floating Cubist planes. If we look at the real thing, or as close as we can get to it—photographs of the *petits métiers* under the Second Empire—we find a confirmation of Picasso's source material: both in an *homme-affiche* and in the image of a cocoa vendor. Once we know the sources in the "*Cris de Paris*" and the Parisian street, Picasso's Cubist Managers look a bit less strange.

The great surprise, though, is the discovery that even that most enigmatic character of *Parade*, the Chinese Magician, was drawn from the *image d'Epinal* and the "*Cris de Paris*." For if we look at the figure under "K," the figure who cries "*Kaolin!*", we find a Chinese porcelain merchant. Although he is unquestionably an anomalous character in this chart of Parisian types, he turns out to have been, in fact, a standard figure in the "*alphabet grotesques*" of the "*Cris de Paris*."[11] His costume and headgear may vary, but he always looks more or less like Picasso's Chinese Magician in *Parade*. Cocteau must have sensed how much this extraordinary presence would appeal to his friend Picasso, who was himself both an exotic fixture on the Parisian scene and the fixed point of reference for all modern endeavor.

In the *image d'Epinal* Jean Cocteau discovered the ideal antidote for the visual "decadence" of the prewar Ballets Russes aesthetic: in place of the oriental, convoluted, and sexually charged, the *image d'Epinal* offered a vision that was French, direct, and childishly innocent. Cocteau had found a primitivism that was not savage, a realism that was not empirical, and a visual form that, although sanctioned by modernism, was not modern. In fact, he had found, in the "*Cris de Paris*" and other

Lepape. *Le Boeuf sur le toit* by Darius Milhaud, Jean Cocteau, Raoul Dufy, Guy Fauconnet, Comédie des Champs-Elysées, 1920

LE BŒUF SUR LE TOIT

Raoul Dufy. *Le Boeuf sur le toit*, 1920

popular prints, an art that in its recent history had appealed first to the Left—in the mid-nineteenth century, when Champfleury, Courbet, and their friends supported the popular arts—and then to the Right, when the *"Vieux Paris"* advocates took up their cause. Yet, for all that Cocteau had found in the *image d'Epinal* his "path of France," his middle road between "taste" and "vulgarity," there is a melancholy in his use of it. We might even say of Cocteau's visual aesthetic, as realized in *Parade*, *Le Boeuf sur le toit*, and *Les Mariés de la Tour Eiffel*, what Cocteau said of the art of his friend La Fresnaye in 1921: that it conveys "the sweet sadness of those who know that the human alphabet offers a limited number of combinations."[12]

Notes

1. Jean Cocteau, "*Les Biches*," 1924, appendix to *Le Coq et l'Arlequin* in *A Call to Order* (New York: Haskell House, 1974), p. 67.

2. Cited in Phoebe Poole, "Picasso's Neo-Classicism, Second Period, 1917-25," *Apollo* 85 (March 1967): 200-201.

Cocoa vendor, street vendor, Paris, Second Empire
Collection Sirot-Angel, Paris

3. Jean Cocteau, *Dans le ciel de la patrie* (Paris: Société Spad, 1918).

4. Cocteau wrote this now-famous phrase (followed by Picasso's name in parenthesis—it was a quotation from the painter) in his so-called *Cahier roman*, the notebook he kept during *Parade*'s rehearsals in Rome. This notebook has been reproduced in full in Richard Axsom's *Cubism as Theater* (New York: Garland Publishers, 1979), an excellent study that is basic to any discussion of *Parade*, as are also Douglas Cooper, *Picasso Theater* (New York: Harry N. Abrams, Inc., 1968) and "The Ballet *Parade*: A Dialogue Between Cubism and Futurism," Marianne Martin, *Art Quarterly*, n.s., Spring 1978.

5. Picasso bought a postcard in Naples with a reproduction of Vianelli's peasant painting (it appears to have been a gouache). It contains at the right a group of revelers very similar to those on the *Parade* curtain, a group of strolling musicians at the left, and is set in a *taverna* on the Bay of Naples, with a view of Mount Vesuvius in the background.

6. Quoted in Francis Steegmuller, *Cocteau, A Biography* (Boston: Little Brown, 1972), p. 138.

7. Frederick Brown, *An Impersonation of Angels, A Biography of Jean*

Cocteau (New York: The Viking Press, 1968), p. 138. Brown's biography is, I think, the least sympathetic and most astute treatment of Cocteau's life and art to date. I have taken the liberty of reverting to Rimbaud's original text and offering my own translation in place of Brown's.

8. Clément Janin, *"Les Estampes et la Guerre," Gazette des Beaux-Arts* 59, 1917, pt. 3, p. 485. For the original *images d'Epinal*, see J. Mistler, F. Blaudez, and A. Jacquin, *Epinal et l'imagerie populaire* (Paris: Hachette, 1961), and for the *"Cris de Paris,"* see Massin, *Les Cris de la Ville, Commerce ambulants et petits métiers de la rue* (Paris: Gallimard, 1978).

9. Cocteau wrote this in 1921 in a letter to Jean Börlin that is reproduced in Musée d'Art Moderne de la Ville de Paris, *Cinquantenaire des Ballets Suédois 1920-1925 (Collections du Musée de la Danse de Stockholm,* 1970), p. 54. Also important for Cocteau's theater of the period is the catalog *Au Temps du "Boeuf sur le toit,"* Artcurial, Paris, 1982.

10. See the *"Cahier roman"* in *Parade*, Axsom, pp. 340 and 363.

11. There is, for example, a *"Loterie Alphabétique des Cris de Paris,"* no. 178, in the collection of the Musée Carnavalet, Paris, where under the letter "Y" one again finds a Chinese porcelain vendor looking much like Picasso's Chinese Magician, wearing a red and yellow tunic and with a long pigtail down the back of the head. Reproduced in Massin, *Les Cris de la ville*, p. 154.

12. Jean Cocteau, *"Autour de la Fresnaye," L'Esprit nouveau*, no. 3 (n.d.): 325.

Jean Cocteau. *The Den of Iniquity*. Illustration from *Dessins*, 1924

A Thousand Flashes of Genius*

Pierre Chanel

D RAWING, IN JEAN COCTEAU'S CASE, is the child of hand-writing. In his album *Dessins* he declares: "Poets don't draw. They unravel their handwriting and then tie it up again, but differently." The calligraphic character of his book dedications and the numberless profiles with which he decorated his letters to friends is unmistakable. These "written" profiles are in the tradition of the figures and ornamentations executed at a single penstroke by calligraphers of the past. And it was surely no accident that his friend Picasso decided to illustrate the original edition of one of Cocteau's earliest works, *Le Coq et l'Arlequin*, with two calligraphic drawings.

Over the years, Cocteau developed his own theory of line. In the chapter of *La Difficulté d'être (The Difficulty of Being)* entitled "*De la Ligne*," he synthesized aesthetics and ethics, reuniting the line of the artist and that of the writer in a single philosophical continuum. "What is line? It is life. A line must

*This essay was translated and adapted by Arthur King Peters from the original article by Pierre Chanel in the October 1983 issue of *Le Magazine Littéraire*, dedicated to Jean Cocteau on the twentieth anniversary of his death. Peters also translated the *Chronology* by Bernard Delvaille, which appeared in the same issue of the magazine.

live at each point along its course in such a way that the artist's presence makes itself felt above that of the model . . . With the writer, line takes precedence over form and content. It runs through the words he assembles. It strikes a continuous note unperceived by ear or eye. It is, in a way, the soul's style, and if the line ceases to have a life of its own, if it only describes an arabesque, the soul is missing and the writing dies. That's why I constantly repeat that the philosophical progress of an artist is the only thing that counts . . ."

Cocteau the draftsman antedates Cocteau the poet, and from adolescence on the precocious flowering of his graphic gifts unfolded. As a child he had drawn cartoons and sketched theater sets long before turning to writing. The Cocteau archives at Milly-la-Forêt contain letters to his grandparents written as early as 1900, when Cocteau was about eleven years old, that were illustrated with his drawings of caves, lighthouses, and interiors of rooms. For Cocteau, to draw, in the later years of scandal, turbulence, and war, was to return to the calm shelter of his early childhood at Maisons-Laffitte, near Paris, where Max Lebaudy, the sugar king, washed down his gleaming carriages in champagne, and when all was still right with the world. In 1962, the year before he died, Cocteau noted on the back of one of his earliest drawings, a portrait of his brother Paul: "I must have been thirteen or fourteen at the time and had an uncanny ability to catch a likeness." During the preliminary stages of work on his first novel, *Le Grand Ecart* (*The Splits*), Cocteau wrote his mother: "It's all written [mentally]. Now I have to *draw* each page, copy it until it catches the likeness, the way I do in my portraits and caricatures." In a 1922 letter he had written: "Drawing greatly amuses me. It's a relief when I'm writing, or *not* writing." This lifelong reciprocal transfer of his creative attention from word to image and back again clearly refreshed him at a deep level, and was central to his creative process.

Cocteau's early study of the caricatures of Sem and Cappiello, two famous cartoonists of the day, contributed to the development of his talents for capturing the essential with a single line. His first published drawings appeared in Paul Iribe's *Le Temoin*

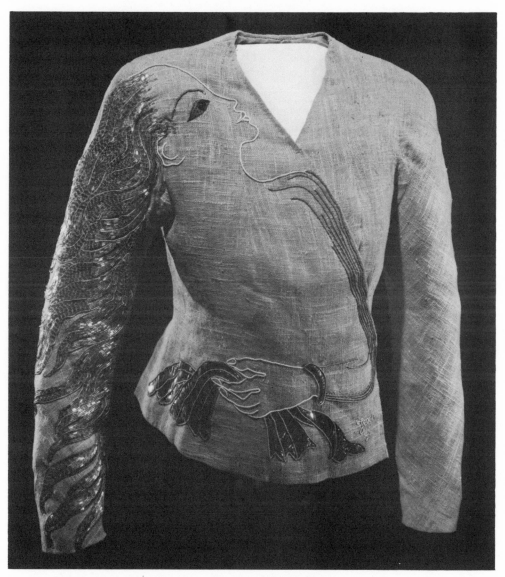

Blue linen jacket, beaded, with embroidery. Designed by Jean Cocteau for
Elsa Schiaparelli, 1935. Philadelphia Museum of Art

Jean Cocteau drawing

and in *Comoedia*. Others followed in 1914–15 in *Le Mot*, a review Cocteau founded and edited with Iribe. But Iribe's elegant presentations, heralding the style of Art Deco illustrations, had little influence on Cocteau's drawing. To the sclerosis of stylization Cocteau always opposed the vitality of *style*, and remained faithful to the incisive manner of his early models. He always cultivated a synthesizing purity of line in his graphic and plastic work, both of which were chiefly concerned with the human face and form.

In childhood Cocteau had contracted "the red and gold sickness" of the theater. No wonder then that he chose as his first subjects Sarah Bernhardt, Edouard de Max, Mistinguett,

Madeleine Carlier (with whom he had a sketchy liaison that later served as the inspiration for his novel *Le Grand Ecart*), the dancers of the Ballets Russes, and particularly Nijinsky, whose artistry and physical presence overwhelmed him. In these first caricatures by Cocteau appears a humorous vein that runs through all his graphic work. They are also fundamental to his work as a portraitist. Forsaking satiric intentions, the caricaturist-turned-portraitist constantly studied the features of his closest friends and tirelessly interrogated his own image in the mirror. His *Mystère de Jean l'Oiseleur* (*The Mystery of Jean the Fowler*) is a collection of thirty-one self-portraits, illustrated by texts. In drawing after drawing he successfully releases the essential line that fixes both the physical likeness and moral truth of the model. This quality is the graphic father of his unique literary style, with its arresting images, the compressed wisdom of aphorisms, and the paradox of oxymorons. Consider his written portrait of Orson Welles, whom he had met in 1936: "Orson Welles is a kind of giant with the look of a child, a tree filled with birds and shadows, a dog that has broken its chain and lies down in flower beds, an active idler, a wise madman." Like so many of his works, whether graphic or written, this is also in part a self-portrait of the artist. From Picasso, Diaghilev, and Stravinsky to Lifar, Kessel, and Genet, each of his portraits of the celebrated writers and artists who were Cocteau's friends and colleagues restores a striking presence that is at once their own and his. Cocteau's art as portraitist culminates in his great study of Colette, without doubt the summit of his graphic art.

Gently ironic and affectionate, without bite or venom, the ensemble of his caricature-portraits makes a serious social and philosophical statement, one that comes not from the artist's head, but rather—typically for Cocteau—from his heart. The caricatures of *Portraits-Souvenir* (*Memory Portraits*), selected flashbacks to Cocteau's childhood, collectively depict not merely one more narcissistic self-portrait of Cocteau, but the interface between pre–World War I Parisian society and its postwar successor, with their evolving heroes and values. Taken together, the caricatures confirm the artist's view of life as theater and theater as life, of beauty and fame as ephemeral. The deceptively free, quick, airy grace of Cocteau's drawing style—with its extensions in film, on the stage, and in the written word—was therefore an appropriate mode of expression. That style itself, so inimitable that he has had no followers, nevertheless expresses some of Cocteau's sturdiest aesthetic convictions: that art is a lie that tells the truth; that beauty, which is always born invisible, lives only an instant; and that for a work of art to be beautiful it must have a moral purpose.

After 1911 Cocteau turned to poster art, with twin triumphs: the posters for the creation of the ballet *Le Spectre de la Rose* (*Specter of the Rose*), featuring Nijinsky and Karsavina. They were followed by many others, and for over half a century

Jean Cocteau. *Vaslav Nijinksky in "Le Spectre de la Rose,"* 1911

Cocteau's extraordinary hand spun out drawings by the thousands with remarkable variety: book illustrations, fashion sketches for Chanel and Schiaparelli, publicity designs, and even the calligraphic profile of Marianne for a French postage stamp. In 1913 Cocteau had not yet met Picasso nor clashed with André Breton, later the High Priest of Surrealism. And Freud had not yet been translated into French. Yet it was in 1913, while writing and illustrating *Le Potomak* (*The Potomac*), that bizarre seedbed for his later works, that Jean Cocteau unearthed both his originality as an artist and the realization that "poetry" (Cocteau's word for the spirit of art in all its forms) resulted from the marriage of the conscious and the unconscious. In *Le Potomak*, the texts, both prose and poetry, are organized around a series of drawings, a curious mutation of the comic strip. They recount the adventures of a peaceful couple named the Mortimers who end up cannibalized by a band of mysterious man-eaters, the Eugènes. The book also describes the spontaneous birth of these monsters under the draftsman's hand as it wandered across a blank page. The critic Milorad underlines Cocteau's role here as a precursor: "His hand, somehow, drew by itself, without conscious direction. Long before the Surrealists' famous 'automatic writing,' Cocteau had invented automatic drawing."

In 1916 he met Picasso, who at the time was turning back to traditional figuration. Picasso's influence on Cocteau's work, however, was more philosophical than formal. His example taught Cocteau the artist's need to break old habits, periodically to shed his skin, in order continually to achieve self-renewal. This led him to use the most varied forms of expression in all his work. When he met Picasso, Cocteau also discovered an entirely new artistic milieu. He invited Raoul Dufy, Albert Gleizes, and André Lhote to collaborate on the final issues of *Le Mot*; spent time with Juan Gris, La Fresnaye, Modigliani, and Lipschitz; became friends with Valentine Gross (also expert at calligraphic drawing) and her husband, Jean Hugo, grandson of Victor Hugo. Nevertheless, Cocteau did not sever his bonds of friendship with such artists as Léon Bakst, Jacques-Emil Blanche, and José-Maria Sert, who linked him to a more classic mode of expression.

After *Le Potomak*, an overview of Cocteau's drawings reveals

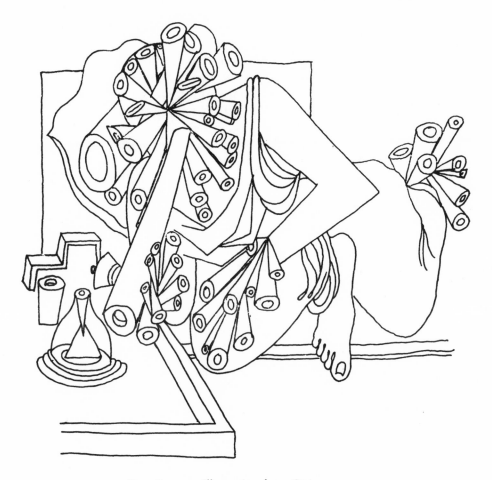

Jean Cocteau. Illustration from *Opium*, 1930

an important body of work created between 1924 and the early 1930s, which consummated once more his marriage of the conscious with the unconscious, this time under the influence of opium. In December 1923, the death from typhoid fever of Cocteau's young protégé, Raymond Radiguet, plunged Cocteau into a deep depression from which he tried to escape through drugs. He executed the 1925 drawings for *Maison de santé* (*Mental Hospital*) and those for *Opium* in 1928–29 during his first two "detoxification" cures. He described these violently Expressionistic drawings as "screams of suffering in slow motion." The imaginary people in the drawings, often depicted as mutilated, convey a sense of panic. Many also reflect the altered perceptions triggered by opium. "The smoker becomes one with the objects around him. His cigarette becomes a finger that drops from his hand." Thus a succession of fantasy figures is born from a combination of conical shapes resembling the opium smoker's pipe.

To Cocteau the drug seemed one way to draw nearer to the heart of mystery, to the invisible, to the netherworld where Radiguet, transfigured as the angel Heurtebise in *Orphée* (*Orpheus*), was to reign as the transcendent hero of Cocteau's personal mythology. That mythology borrowed heavily from Greek myth, in particular the two tragic figures of Oedipus, whose adventure exemplifies "the great enigma of fatal destiny and free will," and of Orpheus, the poet who "tracks the unknown" and penetrates the kingdom of death. Drawing as well as writing set in motion that private mythology whose icons were assembled in *Opéra*, a collection of poems teeming with angels, dreamers, sailors, living statues, and the stars that were from then on an element of his signature, a sort of personal logo.

Yet it is less the philosophical Greece of Sophocles that inspired the magical and dream-related Hellenism of *Opéra* than the metaphysical Greece of Giorgio de Chirico, whom Cocteau hailed as "a painter of the laic mystery." It was this "mystery of the people" that Cocteau tried to make visible through the objects he created in the summer of 1926 at the Hotel Welcome in Villefranche-sur-mer. Those objects were his first attempt at transcending the limits of the graphic. The exhibition catalog, called *Poésie plastique*, recorded the astonishing raw materials used by the artist: thumbtacks, hairpins, candles, matches, lumps of sugar, and stars made of pasta. "From morning to night, from night to morning," he wrote his mother, "I glue, I cut out, I splash paint, I smear pastels, I melt walnut stain, I mix lipstick with sealing wax." These humble objects from everyday life were a methodological confirmation of Cocteau's aesthetic doctrine that one of the artist's tasks was to remove the veneer from commonplace objects and reveal their hidden beauty. Such a process, which stripped the blinders from men's eyes, offered endless possibilities for change and growth, for expanding consciousness. Cocteau's art aimed at making another commonplace object, the average man, aware of capacities that had lain dormant and neglected in him, capacities for uncovering beauty, for becoming, in a sense, an artist himself.

A faithful transcriber of his personal mythology, Cocteau was also the ideal illustrator of his own novels and plays. The merit of his illustrations lies in the distance that separates drawings from texts, thus avoiding redundancy. In the illustrations for *Le Grand Ecart, Thomas l'Imposteur (Thomas the Impostor)* and *Les Enfants terribles (The Holy Terrors)*, it is the extreme economy used to render the story into images that allows full play to the reader's imagination. The illustrations for *Le Livre blanc (The White Book)* stand back from the twists and turns of the narrative and tend toward a sort of exotic Surrealism. In *Orphée* a counterpoint is set up between the text, which modernizes the myth, and the lithographs, which restore it to antiquity. In the *Orphée* lithographs, as in Cocteau's drawings on the unicorn theme, the lyric motion of line triumphantly demonstrates the linear mastery Cocteau had achieved.

The art of wall decoration, which Cocteau had first attempted in the Villa Blanche at Tamaris in 1932, and again in the Villa Croix-Fleurie at Pramousquier in 1937, was an extension of his graphic expression that culminated in the multiform plastic production of the last fifteen years of his life. Two successes mark his work with murals: the decoration of the Villa Santo Sospir, Francine Weisweiller's home on Cap Ferrat, and that of the chapel of Saint-Pierre in Villefranche-sur-mer. At Santo Sospir, as at Villefranche, the energy of the decorator's hand preserves the cursive fluidity of his line, while the dynamic rhythms of the composition dominate the iconography. Other commissions poured in, and one after the other Cocteau decorated the marriage salon of the Town Hall in Menton, the chapel of Saint-Blaise at Milly-la-Forêt, the chapel of the Virgin at Notre-Dame-de-France in London, and the open-air theater at Cap d'Ail.

Jean Cocteau. *La Peur donnant des Ailes au Courage (Fear Giving Wings to*

Cocteau has explained how in 1948 the use of pastel to execute the cartoon for his tapestry *Judith et Holopherne* had helped him move from a graphic to a plastic mode: "I simply rubbed pastel on corrugated paper and saw that it kept me from being purely graphic. I saw that instead of writing, this brought me closer to the painter's trade." Thanks to pastel, Cocteau extended the use he had previously made of color. In his colored drawings of the 1920s and 1930s, *Le Mystère de Jean l'Oiseleur*, the

Courage) (detail), 1938. Phoenix Art Museum, Gift of Mr. Cornelius Ruxton Love, Jr.

illustrations for *Le Secret professionnel (The Professional Secret)*, *Le Grand Ecart*, and *Le Livre blanc*, color covered little of the surfaces. It applied makeup to the forms, creating a kind of phosphorescence around the line. The powdery colors lent themselves to the evocation of imaginary shapes: astrologers, harlequins, Greek maidens, and sleeping men and women. In *Judith* the unrestrained use of color is made magnificently to serve the poetic concept.

In 1950 Cocteau began easel painting, and by 1954 had completed some fifty canvases, which occupy a curious place in his total work. "To paint without being a painter is not easy," Cocteau wryly admitted. "It is important to ask one's self a preliminary question, and then try to answer it. To scrupulously copy an abstract picture idea . . . Despite a lack of knowledge (or foreknowledge), to bring forth a light out of one's self and to let it shine for better or for worse." In these paintings of flowers, portraits, and mythological or imaginary compositions, Cocteau goes as far as possible in using pure colors. Often fragmented by geometric patterns, the colored surfaces enhance each other violently. The same chromatic intensity is to be found again in his 1961 series of *Inammorati*, drawings with colored crayons that rendered the background surface completely opaque.

A tireless worker, Cocteau allowed himself to be further tempted by other plastic forms of expression. Beginning in 1958, following Picasso's example, he designed countless ceramic plates, cups, and vases in which he plays with the contrast between the gleam of enamel and the dullness of terra-cotta decorated with pastel. During the final decade of his life, his holidays in Spain inspired powerful drawings based on the themes of gypsies and bull fighting. In 1962, the year before his death, he drew the sketches for the stained glass windows of Saint-Maximin Church at Metz.

His protean changes of form, not only in art per se but in many other major and minor artistic genres, earned Cocteau the undeserved reputation of a jack-of-all-trades. Yet when he declared, surely with a smile, "I wanted to be the Paganini of the *violon d'Ingres*," he was, in his sometimes facetious way, proclaiming his seriousness of purpose. In his *Démarche d'un poète*

Jean Cocteau. Illustration from Jean Genet's *Querelle de Brest*, 1947 >

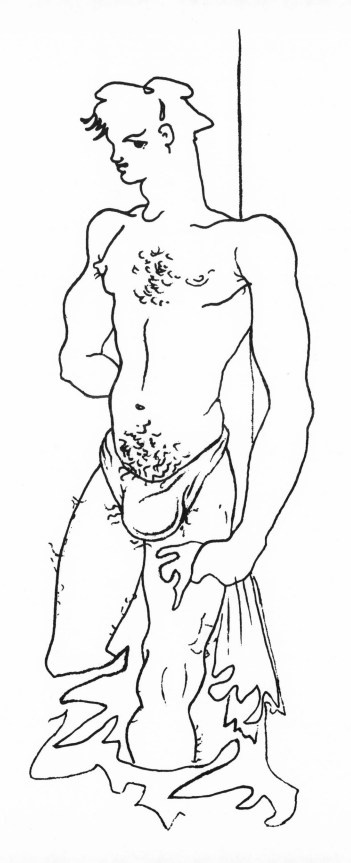

Jean Cocteau. *Memories of the Ballets Russes: Pablo Picasso and Igor Stravinsky*. From *Dessins*, 1924

(*A Poet's Gait*) he asserted: "I never carried out even the least important work carelessly or with my left hand . . . a poet . . . must be capable of everything . . . There is no inn unworthy of the wanderer." Throughout his creative life Cocteau did his utmost to prove that each of the many modes of expression he chose, even the commonplace, could become a privileged medium of poetry.

Cocteau's drawings, usually caricature portraits, were at once teasing and nostalgic. They did not reflect the feelings of alienation, persecution, rebellion, and the feverish search for the shockingly new that characterized so much of his work with visual images in film, theater, and ballet. Such qualities, coupled

Jean Cocteau. *Al Brown*, 1938
Collection Edouard Dermit

with his audacious life style, helped establish Cocteau's reputation as an *enfant terrible* of the arts, as a disturber of the status
quo, and as an avant-garde spirit. Jean Cocteau never stopped
drawing, even in his writing. His written words startle us most
by the rapid series of disturbing images he flashes at us after
painful observation of his outer and inner worlds. Whether
drawn with language or with line, these Cocteau images—most
vividly expressed in his films—have a simplicity and directness,
a complete absence of patina, a purity of style, that preserves
the freshness of their impact and their validity for generations
beyond his own.

Cocteau at the Théâtre des Champs-Elysées during the
production of *Oedipus Rex*, 1952

The Theater of Jean Cocteau

Neal Oxenhandler

MORE THAN ANY OTHER ARTIST OF HIS TIME, Jean Cocteau knew the meaning of theatricality. As a child, he found it in his mother, "bristling with aigrettes and swathed in red velvet" as she prepared to leave for the opera. In his imagination he invented a play based on the counterfeit horror of the Grand Guignol and the splendor of High Mass at his neighborhood church, La Trinité. On his first visit to the theater he saw *Around the World in Eighty Days*. The experience marked him forever. For the rest of his life he experienced *"le mal rouge et or"*—a longing for the red and gold of the theater. He found theatricality in the circus, where he saw the Fratellini clowns and the transvestite acrobat, Barbette. Boxers, fashion mannequins ("like jockeys who are their own horses and perform in a paddock of mirrors"), and of course the stars, those sacred monsters "who possess the secret resources of lightning and its awesome tricks," —all these beings were of the same race as Cocteau.

Cocteau put a proscenium arch around his life. Though he

was at home everywhere, he lived most fully amid the trompe-l'oeil of canvas flats, the hum of lights, the rough indifference of the stagehands, and the smell of dancers' sweat. Cocteau was one of those beings who must dramatize life in order to find out who he is. In the theater he momentarily overcame that "difficulty of being" to which "poetry of theater" was the only possible answer.

Cocteau's work for the theater falls into three periods. First there were the works of "minor beauty"—ballets and adaptations created during and after World War I. Then came the works of the late 1920s and 1930s which (even though sometimes based on the classics) achieved a powerful originality and brought him fame. Finally, the success of these plays allowed him to finance his major films during the 1940s. The plays written during the 1940s, however, tended to be derivative and unconvincing.

Cocteau's first works for the stage were ballets, inspired by his friendship with Nijinsky and Diaghilev. Not only did Cocteau write the plots for these ballets, he intrigued to bring all the artists involved—Picasso, Satie, Auric, Poulenc, Honegger, Milhaud—together in wartime under conditions of extreme duress. Throughout his career, he was to manifest a genius for reconciling difficult personalities. This gives to his work a quality of improvisation and spontaneity. Each work becomes a minor miracle pulled off by bravado and skill.

The ballets represent what Cocteau called "minor beauty," which is full of tricks and surprises. It's found in costume or sleight-of-hand, in puns and plays on words. It's the beauty of the street singer, the nightclub *chansonnier*, the carnival mime. Cocteau associated himself with these self-taught artists as he studied to learn how he might enter the world of traditional French theater. In France, national identity had come to its sharpest focus in the poetic drama of the seventeenth century, with Corneille, Racine, and Molière. The classical tradition defined not only French theater, but French culture itself. Every artist since that time has dreamed of writing for the theater and of being performed at the Comédie-Française, the "house of

Pablo Picasso. *Portrait of Leonid Massine* (choreographer of *Parade*), 1919
The Art Institute of Chicago, Margaret Day Blake Fund

Léon Bakst. *Nijinsky in "L'Apres Midi d'Une Faune,"* 1912. Wadsworth
Atheneum, Hartford, Connecticut, The Gallup Sumner
and Mary Catlin Sumner Collection

Pablo Picasso. *Léon Bakst*, 1922. Musée Picasso, Paris

Molière." In his early works Cocteau displayed an amazing ability to use the *truc*, or trick, whether of language or spectacle. "The *truc*," he once said, "is art itself. Poetry is a vast pun." Clearly, a long moral and artistic development had to be undergone before he could enter the house of Molière.

After the ballets, Cocteau wrote a number of adaptations: *Antigone, Romeo and Juliet, Oedipus the King.* These were streamlined versions of the originals. *Romeo and Juliet* was described by Cocteau as a "pretext for a choreographic production." He directed the play and also played the role of Mercutio. It seemed impertinent of him, to those who dismissed Cocteau as a frivolous jack-of-all-trades, to meddle with Shakespeare's text. But Cocteau had the instinct of a born dramatist who knows that the great works of the past must be reinvented. While stripping Shakespeare's play of much of its verbal lyricism, he added to it a poetry of motion. This use of machines goes back to the Greeks and the *deus ex machina*, the "god from the machine." It had often been a feature of the spectacle plays in the Middle Ages and the Renaissance. But Cocteau added some new touches, inspired by his contacts with Italian Futurism. Not only did the mobile sets decompose and rebuild like a house of cards, but the actors themselves seemed to fly. Romeo, a kind of somnambulist, moved in harmony with an absent music (a technique later adopted by the American choreographer Merce Cunningham). The behavior of the play's protagonists anticipated the unpredictability of those adolescents who would appear in most of Cocteau's later works. Romeo throws a tantrum and Juliet lies on her stomach to talk to Romeo over the edge of the balcony. Cocteau was always a child at heart; it is not surprising that teenagers were to become his favorite heroes and heroines.

Cocteau's work up to this point is characterized by the title of his first ballet, *Parade.* In that ballet gesticulating Managers with immense cardboard heads try to persuade the crowd to come inside their street fair. "The real show is on the inside." But nobody buys a ticket and gets to see. Nor did Cocteau himself, at the start of a long search for identity, know what

Pablo Picasso. Stage curtain for *Parade*, 1917. Musée National d'Art Moderne, Paris

was "inside" in 1917. All he could do was spin images in a constant flow of visual and verbal invention. These spectacular signs float in space, like smoke above a candle. It took Cocteau many years to discover the identity of his deepest self.

Cocteau's thousand and one transformations, his changes of lovers or of moods, his dropping the pen to pick up the camera or the brush—this was more than mere instability. Not only did these experiments hold the secret of new art forms waiting to be born in the 1950s and 1960s, they bespoke an existence that very few men or women can undertake without destroying themselves: the life of pure theatricality. Cocteau remains its chief exponent in the first half of the twentieth century.

French theater in the 1920s divided into two streams. One of these, which tempted Cocteau later in his career, was Naturalism, the theater that attempted to "imitate" life. Sometimes this involved putting a butcher shop, complete with raw meat, on the stage. More often, as in the plays of Ibsen, it meant revealing human motives that were shocking to bourgeois society. The other current, with which Cocteau was more clearly attuned, had come down from Symbolism. It was a theater of atmosphere, of fantasy and invention.

Cocteau, of course, admitted no teachers, except the young novelist Raymond Radiguet, tragically dead at nineteen. But his best theatrical works are pure invention, based on playing tricks with reality.

In 1928 Cocteau wrote to Jacques Maritain that "mystery" was his obsession, his "*idée fixe*." Clearly the path to the exploration of mystery lay not in imitating life but in going behind appearances—even through death itself, as he claimed to do in his first important play, *Orpheus*. Mystery meant many different things to Cocteau in the various stages of his career. In *Orpheus* it meant primarily the supernatural, the realm of the dead, entered through a mirror. "Look in a mirror and you will see death working like bees in a hive." On the other side of the mirror, the dead continue their lives amid monsters and marvels, but the only emotion they display is hostility toward the living.

Orpheus, produced in 1926 by the famous Russian actors

Pablo Picasso. *Women Running on the Beach*, 1922. Musée Picasso, Paris
An enlarged rendition of this painting formed the backdrop
for the play *Le Train bleu*

Georges and Ludmilla Pitoëff, can be seen now in the 1980s as a brilliantly conceived homage to the supernatural. One aspect of Cocteau's genius was his ability to synthesize, to bring together fragments of the past and present, to create momentary unity out of the debris of 2,500 years of Western culture. So the play takes the ancient story of Orpheus, prince of poets. He and his wife, Eurydice, live like some upwardly mobile middle-class couple in a cozy *nouveau* Greek house, designed by Chanel. He writes poetry and is involved in literary one-upmanship with other Thracian literati, who are for the most part mediocre. When his work takes him away from Eurydice, she runs with a gang of wild girls, the Bacchantes.

To complete the eclecticism of the play and to please Jacques Maritain and the Catholic writers and poets who formed a community around the young neo-Thomist philosopher, Cocteau put in a few Christian borrowings. Raïssa, Maritain's wife, has characterized this as the period of *"les grandes amitiés"* (the great friendships) and, although Cocteau could not for long reconcile his way of life with the stringencies of Catholic practice, he always remained a "believer" of sorts. His brief return to Catholicism expressed his search for values beyond the parade. So an angel appears in the play, disguised as a window-mender with a rack of glistening glass panes on his back. When he first appears to Eurydice, he kneels, like the angel Gabriel in Renaissance paintings of the Annunciation.

The scene is the couple's home at Thrace. There is a mirror on the left wall and at stage rear a white horse, protruding from a niche. As the play begins, Orpheus is trying to interpret a message that the horse is tapping out with his hoof. Eurydice expresses her jealousy of this supernatural nag who takes so much of her husband's time. He replies angrily: "This horse enters my life and leaves it like a diver. He brings back phrases from it. Don't you see that the least of these phrases is more astonishing than all the poems in the world? I would give my collected works for a single one of these little phrases wherein I listen to myself as you listen to the ocean in a seashell. Not serious? What do you require, my little one? I discover a world. I turn my skin inside out. I track the unknown."

The horse may be interpreted as the devil, the unconscious, or simply the marvelous. At any rate, the poem he taps out for Orpheus turns out to be a trick. It consists of one line: *MADAME EURYDICE REVIENDRA DES ENFERS* (MADAM EURYDICE WILL COME BACK FROM HELL). Orpheus enters the poem in a contest, but the judges are infuriated because the initial letters of the words when placed together spell *MERDE*.

While Orpheus is at the contest, Eurydice is murdered by her ex-friends, the Bacchantes. Returning, Orpheus decides to rescue her from death. Instructed by the angel, he passes through the mirror. He returns with Eurydice, but life together is impossible, since he is not allowed to look at her. To make matters worse, the Thracian public, led by the Bacchantes, comes to harass Orpheus, claiming that he has submitted an obscene poem.

One scenic trick follows another. Orpheus is decapitated by the Bacchantes. Eurydice leads him back through the mirror. The angel places Orpheus's head on a pedestal, where, in answer to questions from the police, it announces that it is Jean Cocteau and gives Cocteau's address, 10 rue d'Anjou. This apparent intrusion of "reality" into the play does not break the illusion. It mingles daily life with the play's fictions and enhances that sense of complicity between the author and the supernatural that had so possessed Cocteau during the writing of this play. Cocteau tells us that the play is perhaps a fiction, but its truth is real. Didn't he once say of himself that he was "a lie that always tells the truth"? As the play ends, Orpheus, Eurydice, and their angel return to live together in harmony as the set mounts on wires into the loft.

Because of the flatness of the characters, this first major work of Cocteau's was called "superficial." But as always, Cocteau was ahead of his time. He knew that the psychologism of the boulevard plays of Sardou, Bernstein, and Lenormand was phony. He knew that a sense of character in the theater is not created by the typology that defines one man by his having an inferiority complex, or another as a womanizer. The well-made plays that had dominated French theater since the end of the nineteenth century belonged to an exhausted genre. Cocteau's

Man Ray. *Ball at the Château of the Vicomte de Noailles*, 1929
The Vicomte Noailles, an avid supporter of the avant-garde, sponsored the
production of *Le Sang d'un poète*. Man Ray is in the foreground

theater is poetic in exactly the same way as that of his great contemporaries, Giraudoux and Anouilh. All of them show human complexity and open out onto life's mystery. Cocteau's plays also resemble those of Giraudoux and Anouilh in the balance among the parts. Cocteau claimed that he learned this neo-classic sense of form from his young friend Radiguet. Radiguet taught him to walk the tightrope above the pitfalls of eclecticism.

The various impulses of *Orpheus* fuse around its major theme: the genealogy of the poet. The star with which Cocteau signed all his work is shown in the film *The Blood of a Poet* (1932) to be a scar, etched into the poet's shoulder.

Cocteau identified himself as a poet, which meant running the risk of provoking public outrage and even martyrdom, as in the case of *Orpheus*. True, Cocteau bore his share of insults and humiliations, which were magnified by the extreme sensitivity of a fragile ego. But persecution and martyrdom are more than a theme, more than a neurosis in Cocteau's work; they constitute one level of its deep mythic structure. Even after he was elected a member of the French Academy and was honored by Oxford, he always felt that he was working in a kind of psychic no-man's-land and that he belonged to that tribe of *poètes maudits* who are in a deep sense outcasts from the society of their time.

Cocteau's first work to be accepted by the Comédie-Française was *The Human Voice*. Created in 1930 for the actress Berthe Bovy, this monologue for the female voice is more than a curtain-raiser. It shows that Cocteau could create a character wounded in her deepest emotions, not a poet this time but an ordinary woman, speaking in anguish over the phone to her lover. The sets for this play were by the talented designer, Christian Bérard, Cocteau's friend and partner in opium. They worked on many plays together, including the monologue that Cocteau wrote for Edith Piaf in 1940, *Le Bel indifférent* (*The Handsome Hunk*).

The Human Voice was one of the first of several swings that Cocteau was to make in the direction of naturalism. Although fantasy was his homeland, he was able to work successfully in

Jean Cocteau and Christian Bérard during the rehearsals for *Renaud et Armide*, 1943

the much more constricting Naturalist form in which a room is only a room, a voice only a voice. But his success in this genre was limited to the monologues and *Les Parents terribles* (*Intimate Relations*), a play which successfully transposes his adolescent hero into the Naturalist mode. Other works in this genre, such as the heavy-handed mystery story *The Typewriter*, were dismal failures.

The Infernal Machine has always been considered Cocteau's greatest work for the theater. Produced in 1934 by Louis Jouvet, the play appeared within the context of other myth-modernizations, by Giraudoux and Anouilh as well as by Cocteau. This fascination with myth can be attributed in part to the neoclassical revival, initiated a number of years earlier by André Gide and Jacques Rivière, editor of the *Nouvelle Revue Française*. French schoolchildren in the 1930s still read Latin and Greek. Ever since the seventeenth century, Greece had been the mirror image of France; Racine and Corneille had used classical models.

Jean Cocteau saw more in Greece than Giraudoux's famous description, "some goats browsing on marble." Besides a concept of style and the acceptance of homosexual love, Cocteau saw in Greece the ultimate model of "purity." "Purity," like "mystery," has a variety of meanings, but its root meaning in Cocteau's lexicon is similar to what we now call authenticity— being true to one's deepest self. It was courageous of Cocteau to set as his highest goal in life just what seemed most impossible for him to attain. After all, he was the quick-change artist, the man of a thousand faces. How could he be true to himself when it took him all his life to find out who he was?

The story of Oedipus, which has been described as the first detective story, exactly conveyed Cocteau's own search for identity. Oedipus was a man who fled from a horrible prediction—that he would kill his father and marry his mother— only to find that his flight made the oracle come true. At the age of fifteen Cocteau too had run away. He ran away to Marseilles, perhaps to join the navy, perhaps only to try opium and engage in some torrid sexual experimentation. It was the first of his many flights in search of himself. The truth that Cocteau finally

Jean Cocteau. Letter and sketch referring to *Oedipus Rex*
Collection Jeffrey D. Schaire, New York

learned about himself, while in no way as horrible as that which Oedipus found, was equally unexpected.

The play begins with a prologue spoken by Cocteau's resonant voice. (As Molière before him, and Hitchcock and Godard after him, Cocteau made cameo appearances in his own works.)

Lights up, dim. We are on the ramparts of Thebes. Two guards discuss the disasters that have befallen the city; it might be the opening of *Hamlet*. We learn that the ghost of Laïus, their dead king, has appeared to them. Moments later the queen, Jocasta, climbs the stairs to their post. She speaks with "that international accent of royalties." She is followed by her blind adviser, the soothsayer Tiresias. The ghost fails to appear to Jocasta and Tiresias. They leave the ramparts unaware that not far away a young man is racing across the desert toward Thebes.

Already in this collage of borrowings, erudition, and private jokes we hear Cocteau's highly personal style. Everything seems improvised—from the high seriousness of Sophocles to the high camp of incest jokes. It is the voice that holds it all together. Once again the actors are choreographed. Once again Cocteau's voice endows each fragment with the genetic imprint of style.

In the original production Oedipus was played by Jean-Pierre Aumont. In later revivals, the part was taken over by Jean Marais, who for many years was the ideal Cocteau hero. Marais combined strength and vitality with a certain softness, a rounding of the features that endowed him with the beauty of a Renaissance angel. Angels, especially fallen ones, always fascinated Cocteau.

In the desert Oedipus encounters the Sphinx, who has taken the form of a young woman. She winds the arrogant youth in the coils of a spell, words linked around the hidden matrix of power: "Useless to close your eyes, to turn your head; for it is neither by song nor by my glance that I act. But more adroit than a blind man, more rapid than the gladiator's net, more subtle than lightning, more obstinate than a coachman, heavier than a cow . . . I secrete, I draw from myself, I release, I unwind . . . these knots . . . so narrow that it escapes you, so supple that you will think yourself victim of some poison . . . a wire which binds you with the volubility of crazy arabesques of honey which falls on honey."

Cocteau had learned how to court power, and the sphinxes of his life, such as Misia Sert, Coco Chanel, and the Comtesse de Noailles, usually fell victim to his counter-charms, as in the play. The Sphinx is disarmed by Oedipus, and tells him the answer to her riddle. Triumphant, he seizes as his trophy the mask of Anubis, the jackal, and rushes off toward Thebes.

The Sphinx and Anubis are an invention; there is no such fairy-tale fantasy in the Sophoclean model. Yet Cocteau is reaching toward a deep truth. In the fairy-tale the hero slays the monster and marries the princess. The princess, of course, is always mother because the fairy-tale hero is a child. No one before Cocteau had realized that *Oedipus* is a story for children.

In Act III we find ourselves in Jocasta's bedroom, "red like a little butcher shop amid the architecture of the city." Throughout the play, Cocteau tried to achieve a miniaturization of the myth, reducing everything in scale. Later productions of the play have moved it in other directions—toward an exaggeration of its implicit violence and obscenity, or toward a representation of those vengeful gods who have set the "infernal machine" of the plot in motion. I have seen several productions of the play, including one that used projections of monstrous leering faces on a screen above the nuptial bed. In another, the bed was a marbleized altar tilted toward the audience, to which Oedipus and Jocasta were offered like sacrificial victims.

Tiresias visits them to warn Oedipus that the oracles are bad. Oedipus brags that he'll outwit them.

TIRESIAS: Do you think they can be outwitted?

OEDIPUS: I am the proof. And even if my marriage vexes the gods, what are you going to do about your promises, about your liberation, about the death of the Sphinx? And why have the gods pushed me on to this very chamber if this marriage displeases them?

TIRESIAS: Do you claim to resolve in one minute the problem of free will? Alas! Alas! Your power intoxicates you.

The conflict between free will and fatality (the gods) had by this time become the central theme of Cocteau's theater. It was again the question of identity. How can I choose to be myself

Man Ray. *Coco Chanel*, c. 1935

when events and other people conspire against me?

Cocteau's heroes are all threatened by the world or by events they cannot control. These events force them to make choices. Oedipus chooses to run away from the oracle, he chooses to kill Laïus at a crossroads, he chooses to marry Jocasta. He has found the identity for which he unknowingly searched, but the price is high. Jocasta strangles herself, Oedipus punctures his eyes. As the play ends, the sacred scapegoat is led out by his small daughter, Antigone, to wander the world.

This play, which began as a pastiche of *Hamlet*, then seemed at times to be turning into a boulevard comedy, ends as a mystery play. Like all great religious works, it warns us that there are limits. These limits are ambiguous; we know only when it is too late that we have transgressed them. In the age of nuclear threat, mass murder, and terrorism, Cocteau's *Infernal Machine* remains wholly contemporary. It is a play for all time.

The Oedipus that Cocteau gives us as the play ends is greater than any of the roles Cocteau himself played in life. Perhaps it was his sense of style as much as his moral sense that kept him from pursuing beyond excess his own transgressions. But he pursued them far enough to write convincingly about them.

Three other works were produced in the late 1930s, marking this decade as the height of Cocteau's dramatic career. There was his *Oedipus the King*, a streamlined version of Sophocles in the manner of his 1922 adaptation of *Antigone*. This production marked Jean Marais's first appearance in a work by Cocteau.

Oedipus the King was Cocteau's third Oedipean work and was based on his first reworking of the myth, the oratorio *Oedipus Rex* that he wrote for Igor Stravinsky. Produced in 1927 in honor of Serge Diaghilev, the somber Latin text was a notable failure at its first performance. Diaghilev called it "a very macabre gift," and added, in a conversation with Vladimir Nabokov, "Everybody knows I dislike sleeping with women, and that includes old hags like Jocasta, even if she should happen to be my mother." Cocteau was excluded from the production, but managed to participate in later revivals and in the recording of the work. As the speaker of the French-language

prologue, his sonorous voice magnificently frames the performance of Stravinsky's score.

In 1937 Jean Marais played Galahad in Cocteau's magical
evocation of the age of chivalry, *The Knights of the Round
Table*. This play, in which Cocteau sought to elude his "Grecian
mania," pits two old men against each other—the evil magician,
Merlin, and King Arthur, who is seeking to restore peace and
prosperity to his troubled land. But the King is bewitched by
Ginifer, Merlin's valet. Like a valet in Molière, Ginifer continually gets his master into and out of trouble. Ginifer supplies
much of the magic in this delightful work of fantasy. He is never
seen in his own Puckish form, but appears now as Gawain,
now as Queen Guinevere, now as Galahad himself. Galahad's
mission is to restore peace to the land, crushed under plague,
poverty, and famine. Merlin's machinations account for some
of the trouble. Lancelot's adulterous relationship with the queen
is a dangerous transgression that must be paid for by all the
people of the realm.

Galahad arrives at the Round Table, and is dubbed the "All
Pure." His purity, we are told, is the equivalent of poetry. What
this means becomes clear as the play ends. Galahad exposes the
sinister Merlin and makes the Grail appear. He alone cannot see
it. "I will never see it. I am he who makes it appear to others."

The poet is scapegoat and sacrificial victim. His role is to give
insight to the community by purifying its language and reconciling its antagonisms. But to accomplish this, he himself must give
up any possibility of happiness. Through Galahad, Cocteau once
again signals his own membership in the race of *poètes maudits*.
Cocteau's poetry and his theatricality fuse in the interchange-
able characters of Galahad and Ginifer.

The last play of the 1930s is Cocteau's finest work in the
Naturalist vein, *Les Parents terribles*. It seemed to signal yet
another change of direction. In point of fact, the play was writ-
ten in the very popular boulevard style in order to introduce
Jean Marais to a wider public. Shortly after its production in
1938, the play was accused of immorality and expelled from the
Théâtre des Ambassadeurs, which belonged to the city of Paris.
This notoriety brought success, and the play continued to run in

another theater until it was interrupted by the "phony war" and the beginning of the German Occupation.

Cocteau rapidly became a target for Vichyite journalists, who reviled him for an article he had written in defense of the Jews as well as for his homosexuality. The supposed incest theme of *Les Parents terribles* seemed to prove his flagrant immorality. "They go so far as to say that *Les Parents terribles* is responsible for the defeat," he wrote to a friend.

The play has often been compared to the works of the king of boulevard theater, Henry Bernstein. The typical Bernstein play opens with a surprise, followed by three peripeties in each of the play's three acts.

The characters: Yvonne and Georges, parents of Michel; Léonie (Léo), Yvonne's sister, secretly in love with Georges; and a young woman named Madeleine. Act I shows us Yvonne's room, lit by a small bedside lamp and by sinister light from the building next door. Bathrobes and nightgowns lie on the floor. The room, like that of the children in Cocteau's novel *Les Enfants terribles (The Holy Terrors)*, reveals a family in disorder. The opening *coup de théâtre* is the discovery by Léonie and Georges that Yvonne, a diabetic, has nearly killed herself with an overdose of insulin. She is frantic with worry over Michel, who has spent the night away from home. The plot builds rapidly, with that repressed intensity so typical of what Freud called "the family romance."

Michel returns home, radiantly happy. He is in love with a young woman, has spent the night with her. His mother claws him in jealousy. The act ends with the awful discovery that Madeleine, Michel's fiancée, is also the mistress of his father.

The play's effectiveness does not lie merely in the demonstration of Sartre's famous line, "Hell is other people" (especially if they happen to be related). Merely tightening the screws on a group of characters is a common theatrical device. The difference is that Cocteau does it in a bravura style. Even within the Naturalist formula, the dialogue is built around metaphors:

LÉO (next to Yvonne, holding her still): Another thing, Yvonne. Our worst suffering comes from being unable to imagine the place where those we love avoid us. Aren't you curious about that woman whom Mik used to hurt you, even though you can't give a precise name to that hurt? If an object is stolen from you, don't you try to imagine where it's hiding?

No doubt the concept of jealousy here comes from Proust, with the incestuous feature added by Cocteau. But the dramatization of that jealousy, the way Yvonne is manipulated by her sister to accept the visit to Madeleine—this moves past psychology into metaphor.

In Act II the family, or "gypsy caravan," as they call themselves, goes to visit Madeleine. Michel, innocent and unknowing, assumes the visit to be friendly. But his mother and father, each for his/her own reason, intend to destroy the relationship. Georges threatens Madeleine. He will reveal the truth to Michel. She has no alternative but to tell Michel that she is in love with somebody else. He leaves in despair, a mood swing that signals the play's second peripety.

In Act III the peripeties succeed each other like explosions. Michel is out of his mind with despair. His mother commits suicide. The young couple may find happiness after all—they have passed through the country of disorder. The doorbell rings. Léonie goes to answer.

LÉO (returning): It was the cleaning-lady. I told her that there was nothing to be done here, that everything was in order.

Jean Marais's acting of the part of Michel, both in the play and the film version, made it clear that he had mastered the entire repertory of Cocteau's heroes. Not only could he portray the abstract beauty of a mythic hero, he could also express the full range of emotions required in Naturalistic acting.

The plays of the 1940s included *Les Monstres sacrés* (*Sacred Monsters*), a vehicle for Yvonne de Bray about actors. Although it has had several revivals, it was never a notable success. In 1941 *The Typewriter* was little more than an unfortunate echo of Henry Becque's great play, *The Crows*. Both deal with anonymous letters and provincial life, but Cocteau was too much of an urbanite to convey the underside of rural life.

At fifty-one, Cocteau was beginning to discover the limits to his versatility. This did not, however, prevent him from writing a tragedy in verse on a theme from the Italian poet, Tasso. The play, *Renaud et Armide*, written entirely in alexandrine verse, was produced at the Comédie-Française in 1943. The action of the play, which takes place in an enchanted garden, recounts the love of the soldier-hero, Renaud, for the siren, Armide.

Cocteau had written verse since childhood, and the poetry of this play was no mere pastiche of French neo-classicism. The plot was traditional—the torments of love in an enchanted garden. But within these constraints, Cocteau evoked a view of love that was thoroughly modern. The enchanted garden became the symbol of all those obstacles to love that Cocteau himself had experienced. The danger of mere infatuation, the inability to find privacy, and the fear, familiar to all celebrities, of being used by parasites. But the chief threat to love lies in oneself. How can love achieve stability when the self is constantly changing?

Armide says, "I want to flee far from myself on this horse of love." The play is dominated by images of escape and flight. For Cocteau the only possible escape was into the flux of poetic language. Pure poetry, invented earlier by Mallarmé and Valéry, represented an escape into the world of ideas. But for Cocteau, pure poetry meant rather the escape into an infinite series of masks.

The spell is finally broken, and Renaud leaves Armide to do battle against the infidels. In this work, whose value has never been fully appreciated, Cocteau proved himself once again the greatest collagist of his time. He could mingle a Petrarchian poetic style with neo-classical theatrical conventions and combine them with ancient myths and a Proustian view of love. The result is a work of soaring style in which the poetic images extend and enhance the effect of sets, lights, and rigorous acting in the style of the Comédie-Française.

As the decade of the 1940s drew to an end, Cocteau made two final attempts to win back his place in the theater. His two historical plays, *L'Aigle à deux têtes* (*The Eagle with Two Heads*) (1946) and *Bacchus* (1951), were attempts to deal with political reality. Although both plays were set in Germanic countries split by unrest and rebellion, the reference to postwar France was unmistakable.

L'Aigle portrays a fanciful queen who has lost all interest in life until she falls in love with a poet, Stanislas. He is pursued into her room by the queen's own guards (once again, a hunted poet). The poet and the queen, the two-headed eagle, struggle to ward off the evil designs of the queen's enemies. The play is political in a negative sense. Cocteau seems to be saying, people such as these, who live in the realm of imagination, should not be called upon to take responsibility. They do not deal with reality—they invent it. He is defending not only poets but mythomaniacs, beings whose theatricality is a kind of detour to the truth.

From the very beginning of his career, Cocteau had been accused of lacking seriousness. Now, in the early 1950s, Jean-Paul Sartre was making his plea for political *engagement*. Cocteau had no interest in building a classless society or bringing about a revolution; such programs in fact made him uncomfortable.

Bacchus was his answer to these ideas. It tells of a young man, the village idiot, who is crowned Bacchus for one day and given the privilege of ruling the city. In fact no idiot at all, he takes over and tries to bring about essential reform. Despite his idealism and heroic strength, he is killed as the result of political intrigue. The hero and heroine of *L'Aigle* had also shown that poets' gifts lift them above the world of politics. When out of generosity they traffic with this world, it turns on them and kills them.

Cocteau's play seemed hackneyed when compared to the complex moral issues presented in Sartre's *Le Diable et le bon Dieu* (*The Devil and the Good Lord*), which was produced at the same time. Cocteau defended himself with his usual paradoxes: " . . . my engagement was in myself and not exterior to me." Or as Hans, his hero, puts it: "To engage oneself in a party is a comfort, since that party supports us and spares us the anguish of nuances to the advantages of a single color."

These words were published in 1951. Since that time, French artists have abandoned most of their external commitments.

Cocteau and the Japanese Kabuki Theater, 1955

The French writers of today would brush aside Cocteau's defense. For them, the "self" is simply another construct of the bourgeois authority system. The emphasis of recent French writers is precisely where Cocteau always placed it—on the sign itself: the word, the *truc*, the trick of language, be it the language of film or of poetry. The radical quality of Cocteau's film language has made him one of the most admired forerunners of modern cinema. While the avant-garde of 1945 scorned Cocteau, a decade later he was honored by the brilliant young filmmakers of the New Wave. So it was perfectly fitting that in 1963 François Truffaut should give the prize money from his first feature film, *The Four Hundred Blows*, to Cocteau for the production of that artist's last film, *The Testament of Orpheus*.

Cocteau's last work for the theater was written for the actors of the Comédie-Française, who had now become his neighbors. He would often visit with them on his way home up the narrow rue Montpensier.

This brief work, called *L'Impromptu du Palais-Royal*, brings Molière and Louis XIV themselves out of the gloom of history. There, on the stage of Molière's own theater, they gossip and argue with a variety of dukes, marquises, and other hangers-on, including that notorious gossip, Saint-Simon.

Here, in a brief soliloquy, Cocteau evokes "the great century" as the time when theatricality was at its peak. Dancing and playacting were the very mode of courtly life. Everything, from the king's first waking to the after-dinner violins, was part of the great play of existence: "Dance, gentlemen. Let one of the minuets that accompanied our revels give you the beat. Yes, my friends, we had the best of it. . . . Dance, one leg on the ground, the other in a dream. Dance between heaven and earth. . . . Dance on the strings our invisible author manipulates overhead."

Cocteau has passed through the mirror, but the marionettes he left behind still dance his dramas and his endlessly inventive dreams.

Jean Cocteau and *Les Six* (left to right: Francis Poulenc, Germaine
Tailleferre, Louis Durey, Cocteau, Darius Milhaud, Arthur Honegger—
Georges Auric is included in the sketch), 1931

Cocteau and Music

Ned Rorem

"**W**HY DO YOU WRITE PLAYS, the novelist asks me. Why do you write novels, the playwright asks me. Why do you make films, the poet asks me. Why do you draw, the critic asks me. Why do you write, the artist asks me. Yes, why, I ask myself. Doubtless so that my seed will be sown where it may. I know little enough of the spirit that is in me, but it is not a tender one. It cares nothing for sickness, nothing for fatigue. It profits by my talents. It seeks to give form to the trumpets . . ."

"Form to the trumpets." What a fortunate phrase—and somehow a trifle sad. Form was an element that Jean Cocteau innately contained, but the trumpets themselves (though he ran, as he liked to say, "faster than beauty") were beyond his grasp. Elsewhere he states: "It is rarely admitted that one can be a poet and a painter, that one can change branches on the same tree. I just heard Charles Chaplin say on Radio Nice that he liked living in France because a man like me could create a poem, a novel, a ballet, sets, costumes, plays, films, a chapel, without being asked

to justify his activities, and without having to specialize . . . Free,
that is the word. I am free—insofar as the night self that rules
me warrants. For alas, I long to be a composer, and what Beethoven in a letter to his publisher about *Fidelio* calls 'the science of
art' prevents me."

Unlike specialized America, where a podiatrist for the left foot
refers you to an associate if it is your right foot that ails you,
Europe has always been a land of general practitioners, and this
is nowhere more evident than in the arts. Yet of even the grandest
Mediterranean G.P.'s, from Leonardo to Sacha Guitry, none
has included musical composition among his accomplishments.
Across the Channel I do count three: Gerard Manley Hopkins,
although his efforts seemed dull and primitive; Noel Coward,
although, proud of his inability to read notes, he improvised
to a stenographer; and Charlie Chaplin—so adored by Cocteau
—although his forays appear restricted to *Limelight*. (Ezra
Pound, after his anglicization, did compose a full-length opera
on Villon, musically original but too coarse technically to be
practicable.) In France, however, where composers have sometimes been professional writers, no professional writer has ever
composed, not even that most famous of all *bricoleurs*, Jean
Cocteau.
   If the one craft that he did not profess was music, he did
bemoan the deficiency, unlike many another fine *littérateur* who
"does without" without apology. Other fine ones, meanwhile,
have countered their inability to write music by writing about
music. None, at least in his fiction, has succeeded (assuming art
about art can ever succeed) as convincingly as our better critics;
they leave their musical readers smiling uncomfortably. Proust
is an *amateur de luxe*; Mann, a conscientious researcher; Rol-
land, a romanticizer. Auden, Pound, Gide, and even Shaw, when
writing on the realities of the musical world, still write as tour-
ists, from the outside; beneath their subtle grandeur they have
no more to say than any well-trained sophomore.
   Despite appearances, France has never been musical. Which is
to say that while producing her share of good composers, plus a
number of great performers—performers unable, however, to

interpret their own composers as well as foreigners do—she has never produced a viable public for these musicians. Indeed, music was officially banned (along with homosexuality) by Breton's Surrealists. If the seven lively arts in the countries of our earth can be distinguished as either aural or visual (and they can: no fine art—cooking and sex are not counted among them—is dedicated to the senses of taste, touch, and smell), the French have always been leaders in the visual. Is it glib to add that the French like to talk about music more than they like to listen to it?

Jean Cocteau, aware of and hurt by these generalities, had two trump cards that the others lacked. Music continually colored his prose and poems, but they inevitably reflected situations rather than constructions, social rapport with makers and their audiences rather than the "creative process." He did not write *about* music, but *around* it, and was careful to subtitle *Le Coq et l'Arlequin* as *Notes autour de la musique*. Also, more than any other writer who ever lived, Cocteau worked *with* musicians; but for him, a great deal of worthwhile music would never have come into being. In collaboration as in commentary, he was canny: hot in the public fray, he remained cool in the joint harness. Whether his prewritten verse was being molded to song or whether he was concocting words expressly to be sung, he left decisions about singability to the composer; unlike Auden, he did not try to aid the composer with "musical" words. Similarly with nonverbal ballet scenarios or with movies and plays needing background music, timing and genre were the composer's decisions. Surely the sharpest lesson Cocteau learned from Diaghilev was that mixed media, to jell and endure, must be made of autonomous components. Which is why *Petrouchka* or *Tricorne* come down to us through their independent ingredients, why Cocteau's texts, Auric's music, and Picasso's sets can stand alone, and why no ballet from any country during the past quarter century has willed us a score of equal quality.

Is it not less astonishing that Beethoven composed while deaf than that he composed great music while deaf? Is it not less astonishing that dolphins talk than that what they utter is worth heeding? Is it not less astonishing that Cocteau now walks with the other immortal multi-talents than that he should have out-stripped them by absorbing the alien art of music into his practice? None of his colleagues, with exception of *Persephone* (a libretto by Gide for Stravinsky), wrote memorable livrets.

"When I admire a painter, people tell me, 'Yes, but that's not painting.' When I admire a composer, people tell me, 'Yes, but that's not music.' When I admire a playwright, people tell me, 'Yes, but that's not theater.' When I admire an athlete, people tell me, 'Yes, but that's not boxing,' and so on. Then I ask, 'But what is it?' My interlocutor hesitates, eyes fixed in space, and murmurs: 'I don't know . . . it's something else.' I have finally realized that this *something else* is, after all, the best definition of poetry."

Nicely contrived, but contrived all the same, since he avoids the sequence "When I admire a poet, people tell me, 'Yes, but that's not poetry.' " Still, we know what he means; and what he termed poetry covers everything he touched—including poetry. Had he (as he put it) "unraveled his words" onto a musical staff, would his Nocturnes have fallen into the same over-all category?

The two artists Cocteau most frequently cites in conversation—the two he is most anxious to let you know he knows—are neither of them poets; Picasso and Stravinsky.

What did Stravinsky teach him? Sobriety, says Jean. "At nineteen, flattered and feted, I had become ridiculous and squandering, a chatterbox taking my own banter for eloquence and my wastefulness for prodigality." His meeting with the Russian composer seems, remarkably, to have been his first brush with someone who took his own work seriously. Cocteau determined to emulate the master of *Le Sacre*. The master, on his side, found the younger man's attraction to his ballet to lie mainly in its aura of scandal. Indeed, the impulse behind Cocteau's emulation, *Parade*, surely lay more in provocation than in expression. As late as 1963, a few weeks before his death, Cocteau was still declaring: "Stravinsky says, 'One must turn the pillow when it becomes warm.' You have to find a fresh

Man Ray. *Igor Stravinsky,* c. 1925

place on the pillow. I often change my means of expression to let the vehicle rest, or it clogs . . ." He seems to have forever missed the *musical* point of Stravinsky. He wrote: "I have often heard *Le Sacre* without the dances. I would like to see it with the dances. In my memory, impulse and method balanced each other in the choreography, as in the orchestra. The defect consisted in the parallelism of music and movement, in their lack of interplay, of counterpoint. Here we had the proof that the same chord, often repeated, is less fatiguing to the ear than the frequent repetition of a single gesture to the eye. People laugh at a monotony of automatons rather than at a breakdown of attitudes, and at the breakdown of attitudes rather than at the polyphony from the pit."

Yes, but is the same chord really the same, since each repetition occurs within a constantly shifting asymmetrical rhythm, and the chord's "meaning" shifts accordingly? And is the polyphony really polyphony, since Stravinsky was not a polyphonist? Yet Cocteau is right to intuit (as I believe he is doing) the ambiguity, if not the outright failure, of *Sacre* as a spectacle. Of course, the final reason that *Sacre* has never worked as a ballet—and I say this with the hindsight unavailable to Cocteau—is because its choreographers take it at face value. Choreography that interprets music on the music's terms is asking for trouble. Dance must go against the music.

Now he hits the nail on the head: "Stravinsky does not yield to the danger of autointoxication, of making himself beautiful or ugly. He transforms raw power, devising for its use apparatus ranging from factory to flashlight . . . He composes, dresses, talks the way he pleases. When he plays the piano, he and the piano fit: one object; when he conducts the *Octet*, he turns his astronomer's back on us to solve this magnificent instrumental problem with silver figures."

Oedipus Rex, a "visual" oratorio that became their birthday gift to Diaghilev in 1927, was the sole collaboration of Cocteau and Stravinsky. It was also the first of Cocteau's three treatments of the legend (*Oedipe-Roi* and *The Infernal Machine* were the others), and his most significant foray in tandem with a musician.

". . . music distracts us less from a spectacle than a spectacle keeps us from hearing . . ."

An artist is never wrong—at least never so long as the essays of his artistry are concerned—if he is a "true" artist and if the particular essay catches fire (for not every essay, even from a genius, lives and breathes). By the same token, an artist is never right. Right how? Who are we to deem that the added shadow, the substituted semiquaver, the omitted clause on the last page, make all the difference? Right and wrong are moral concepts, and art aims elsewhere.

This notion, worded more wittily, might be worthy of Jean Cocteau, who well knew in his secret heart—which was none too secret—that what he touched did not always turn to gold. (To Julien Green, before sketching his portrait: "My hand's not winged every day.") One generation's sweetness turns sour in the next; Hindemith and Hahn have faded today, Creston and Crumb will fade tomorrow. Cocteau was wrong about Satie, or right for the wrong reasons.

Like other great poets who by definition have a way with the written word—that is, an ear for what is seen—Cocteau paradoxically had not the gift of tongues. Many French of his time and class, depending upon whether they had nannies as children, or upon which way they thought the war would swing, knew a bit of English or German, but Cocteau had none of either, nor was he embarrassed by the lack. This is true of many musicians as well. It does not follow that those with a "musical ear" have the knack for a foreign language. Some of our best composers never get the hang of it, while many a fool speaks many a language with unaccented fluency, and with the same foolishness in each.

Contrary to the universal claim about the universal language, music crosses frontiers less easily than books or pictures, and music seems to be the art least appreciated by other artists. The two-piano team, Fizdale and Gold, recall Cocteau asking them to record the background for a film he was planning in 1949: they were to improvise jazz variations on "Japanese Sand-

man"—or rather, one endless variation that would serve as
soundtrack for the entire movie. Reluctantly they confessed that
they had no gift for jazz. "But you're Americans, aren't you?"
was Cocteau's thunderstruck reply. Yet if he had neither an ear
nor an eye for music, he did have a nose for it, and that nose
was infallible in sensing how music could embellish his own art.
The score that ultimately garnished the movie in question, *Les
Enfants terribles (The Holy Terrors)*, was the Four-piano Con-
certo of Bach-Vivaldi, the first use of Baroque incidental music
in films, and hauntingly right. This was the only Cocteau film
(actually directed by Melville) not to use a score by Georges
Auric. As for the conception in 1928 of the novel *Les Enfants
terribles*, the author says it was written in seventeen days without an erasure, "under the obsession of the song 'Make Believe,'
from *Showboat*; if you like this book, buy the record of the
song, and then reread it with the volume turned up high."

When I finally moved from Paris to New York, certain people
asked, "How well did you really know all those dead French
people?" I noted that to "know well" means an exchange
between two participants of permanent portions of themselves.
In the five or six meals I had with Cocteau, the even fewer with
Eluard, in certain street encounters with green-eyed strangers
who took me by the hand to painful hotels, in tearful chance
meetings with Tchelichev or a hilarious single supper with
Latouche, I felt a contact, a generosity, a participation, a warmth,
a curiosity, an indelibility that permits me to say I knew, and
know, and will always know them well. Meanwhile I'm indiffer-
ent to some people I've seen daily for twenty years; they offer
neither growth nor anecdote. To "know" has to do with intensity, not habit.

Looking back, I see that the young American artist in long-
term French residence during the 1950s was rare, and that the
fact of such an artist was anathema to the insulated French,
even to Jean Cocteau, who prided himself on catholicity. Thus I
see too that their interest in me lay mainly in my interest in
them.

Despite a notoriously accurate memory, I can't remember

how many times I was in the private presence of Jean Cocteau. (We wrote letters until he died, but I do know that we never met again after 1957, when we chatted beside the fireplace at Dugardin's party for the Poulenc opera in June.) Is this due to his so frequent bows? to his tutoyéing of whole audiences which necessarily included me? or to what many termed his enchantment, which wasn't enchantment but largesse? (Genet: "He does not 'charm,' he is charmed. He is not a wizard, he is bewitched . . .") Cocteau was among the handful of giants—Nadia Boulanger, Frank O'Hara, Noel Coward were others—who, when with you, whatever the circumstances, behaved as though you were the one person alive. Such behavior is so special that we recall it as a magic virtue.

Did he know my music? Although he designed two covers for my songs, he never, to my knowledge, heard anything beyond a ballet I played for him in Grasse during the early spring of 1952. This audition was touching to Jean in two ways. First, it took place *chez* Marie-Laure's mother, Marie-Thérèse Bischofsheim, later the spouse of Francis de Croisset, librettist for the operettas of Reynaldo Hahn, who, in turn, had been the composer for Cocteau's theater debut, *Le Dieu bleu (The Blue God)*, just forty years ago that April. Second, my ballet was on the scenario drawn by Jean Marais from *Dorian Gray*, mounted the following month in Barcelona, with sets and costumes by Marais, who also mimed the role of the progressively decaying portrait. (My score today lies in the bottom of a trunk where it shall forever remain.)

During our first meeting, in the red apartment on rue Montpensier, he maneuvered the conversation around music. "Music's not just in the concert hall. That workman out there—he's whistling the start of *Sacre*." The workman was in fact whistling "*La Vie en rose*," but since that tune derives from *Sacre*, the point was proved.

Was his speaking voice musical? Was Bernhardt's golden? Aesthetics change each generation, as do musical trends and even sexual appeal. Contrapuntal and harmonic periods alternate, are seldom simultaneous; plump is in when thin is out; elocutionary elegance is ridiculed by hipsters. Yet who recalls exactly? It's not the contradiction between many people's reports, as in *Rashomon*, but one's own reaction at different stages. His speech (like Bernhardt's, as recordings indicate) was high pitched, nasal, machine-gun fast, stemming so far as I can judge from upper-class fin-de-siècle timbres, and emphasizing, like many of that class, male and female, an anglicized nongutteral "r."

Isak Dinesen once pictured an influential poet as he stands on a bridge preparing his suicide, when along comes a sycophant who begins to ape his gestures. "Ah, must even my dying gasp become the *dernier cri*!"

Yet who bequeaths what? Cocteau declared in my presence—at Robert de Saint Jean's on May 15, 1952, at around 1:30 p.m., to be exact—that it was in Péguy that he found the phrase: We must know how to go too far.

His star became for Marie-Laure de Noailles a leaf, for Louise de Vilmorin a clover, and hundreds of students learned that to be a poet meant merely to have a signature. For me the star becomes here an asterisk betwixt aphoristic paragraphs, since to write of Cocteau is to write like Cocteau.

Stars between paragraphs, but no longer in my eyes. Jean Cocteau was one of the four or five driving forces of my youth (Virgil Thomson was another, my parents, Paul Goodman, the ghost of Ravel), from the moment David Sachs lent me *Les Enfants* in 1938. Since then I have often changed my mind, never my taste. I reappraise Cocteau today in a harder light, discovering that *his* taste, specifically in music, was sometimes mediocre. The harder light is nonetheless a light of love.

When people ask if I ever met *Les Six*, I always enjoy answering, "Yes, I knew all five of them." It was they whom Cocteau lists in these alexandrines:

> *Auric, Milhaud, Poulenc, Tailleferre, Honegger,*
> *J'ai mis votre bouquet dans l'eau d'un même vase . . .*

The vase was a ballet, *Les Mariés de la Tour Eiffel (The Wedding on the Eiffel Tower)*, to which they all contributed music.

Louis Marcoussis. *Darius Milhaud*, 1936. Musée National d'Art Moderne, Paris

The overture and ritornellos dealing with the comings and goings of certain characters were by Georges Auric. Francis Poulenc composed *The General's Discourse* as well as an episode, *The Bathing Beauty of Trouville*, and Germaine Tailleferre, *The Quadrille of the Telegrams*. Darius Milhaud wrote a giddily violent fugue pastiche called *Massacre at the Wedding* (on one of the platforms of the Eiffel Tower), and Arthur Honegger, the *Funeral March of the General*. The sixth composer, Louis Durey, had already withdrawn from the band (but their title stuck) when all this was premiered in 1921 by the Swedish Ballet at the Théâtre des Champs-Elysées.

Thirty-two years later, on November 4, 1953, Jean Cocteau stood before a capacity crowd in the same theater to evoke the remote and golden 1920s of *Le Groupe des Six*, which he took credit for having formulated. That autumn evening in Paris now also seems golden and remote, falling as it does midpoint between the period and place evoked, and the period and place where I write these words, in Nantucket, October 1981. What I once retained of the occasion was clarity and wisdom, and how satisfied I was as a young American to be seated with Marie-Laure in a loge among these "names" with whom I was on cordial terms. (Honegger had taught me during a Fulbright season at the Ecole Normale in 1951–52; Poulenc, whom I'd met on arrival in 1949 through his biographer, Henri Hell, was, remotely yet gently, mentor and model; Georges and Nora Auric were daily friends during the long summer months in Hyères; while Darius and Madeleine Milhaud, whom I was to know better in California during the next decade, were already staunch acquaintances.) Now to reexperience that speech is to hear it as deliciously specious and—would he agree?—*démodé*.

I am aware of the dangers in what we find outmoded. All art is locatable, for all art dates from the moment it is made, the good as well as the bad. The *Pietà* and *Sacre* date well, the *Gleaners* and *Scarf Dance* date cloyingly. Who knows but what, in the shade of millenniums rather than of mere centuries, Beethoven himself might appear not "all that good"? Aspects of collaborative ventures can date at different speeds, as a good old movie whose background music, once so stimulating, now seems to stifle the action. (Witness the ever-vivid Bette Davis in, for example, *The Letter*, hampered by Max Steiner's preemptive leitmotivs.) Even one's own vantage is slippery. I used to dislike cats; now I love cats and am suspicious of anyone who dislikes them. If notions I once penned about Cocteau now make me cringe, surely my words about him today will soon be dated too . . . Meanwhile, before that capacity crowd: ". . . the privilege of the group called *Groupe des Six* was that it was a grouping less of an aesthetic than of a friendly nature. No shadow ever troubled our mutual understanding. This came about because our understanding was based more on feelings than on opinions. If there was a certain general tendency, it might have been toward rescuing the melodic line, a bit drowned by harmonic masterpieces. Each worked in his own manner, no one had edicts to obey. Six artists liked one another, and in me they found a seventh. And there's the entire doctrine of the group . . ."

So far so good, as a clean statement of purpose. However: ". . . It is only fitting to salute Erik Satie. He was not one of the Group, but his melodic line, so pure, so reserved, so noble, was always our school . . ."

Time has proven Satie to be among the most overrated of the underrated masters. But we must earn the right to declare him overrated, as to declare him a master. *Socrate (Socrates)* is among the timeless monuments, and the only important work of Satie. Yet ask any Satilophile or phobe, as they sound off about *Mercure* or *Parade* or the aimless piano solos, how well they know *Socrate*, and they will adopt a glazed stare. Cocteau's overcompensation on behalf of Satie was his glazed stare: he didn't know *Socrate*.

". . . *The Rite of Spring* set up against our young shrubs the strength of a growing tree, and we should have had to admit that we were beaten, had not Stravinsky, sometime later, come over to our methods, and had not the influence of Erik Satie become mysteriously perceptible in his work . . ."

To claim that Stravinsky had "come over" to Cocteau's methods, and had been "mysteriously" influenced by Satie, is not only to rewrite history, but to demean both Stravinsky and *Les Six*, each one of whom had his own identity. As for Satie, he is perhaps the one composer who does not "date," his work lying—"mysteriously"—outside of time (ask an unalerted listener to situate *Socrate*, and he will answer: ancient Greece, Gregorian Italy, a Beatles background), while Stravinsky's music is nothing if not the very definition of its age.

". . .The young musicians of 1953 therefore owe it to themselves to contradict a new kind of counter-charm. It is understandable that they take their stand on Schoenberg and find in him an arm against works that fear his science of numbers . . ."

This is a layman's aside, compatible with the moment. Earlier that year at the Théâtre Marigny took place the first of Boulez's celebrated Domaine Musicale concerts, sponsored by Jean-Louis Barrault, who, in introducing the series, bent Rimbaud's *Il faut être absolument moderne* to suit his *à la page* purposes. Except for Stravinsky's *Renard (The Fox)*, mimed as a refreshing dessert by Barrault himself, the program was strictly German: a grandiloquent Stockhausen, the wooliest Henze, and other deadly serious serial excursions. Wild applause. Cocteau, perplexed, approving the music but not the reaction, exclaimed, "But why do they react that way?" "How would you have them react, *cher maître?*" "Why, they should be booing—*mais qu'ils huassent!*" Again, as I see it now, he was right, but for the wrong reason.

". . . Our group had its flower in a woman, a girl, a musician. Strange as it may seem (since every woman is sensitive and good at figures), although there are many composers with feminine souls—Chopin remains the best example—there is, so to speak, no real woman composer. I salute Germaine Tailleferre as a charming exception . . ."

Well, Shakespeare too uttered things about women that we now find naive and brutal. The so-called feminine soul—currently so unpopular a concept—has never been defined. Yet Cocteau would almost certainly have defined himself as a feminine soul, although, notwithstanding his famous compassion and longing to be loved, he was—currently so popular a concept—a sexist. The eloquent lines from *Le Secret professionel (The Professional Secret)* to the effect that the greatest art triumphs over our intelligence when sexuality speaks, and if "this moral erection does not occur, the pleasure a work of art affords is of a merely

Pablo Picasso. *Erik Satie*, 1920. Musée Picasso, Paris

Platonic or intellectual order and without the slightest elective value"—these lines, though narrowly true, cannot pertain to a *woman's* appreciation of art. Yes, Cocteau does allow that "one might say of a work of art: 'I've got it under my skin,' as a man will say of a woman, or a woman of a man," yet he does not add: or a man of a man, or a woman of a woman. And we poor musicians sigh when he omits us from "those persons whom the least comma in a sentence, the lightest touch of a paintbrush, the merest indentation of a sculptor's finger will put in a state where a higher sexuality prevails." What about the slightest inflection of a sonic sequence, like the *petite phrase* in Vinteuil's sonata? But Cocteau only writes about music when he is writing about music; as with most authors, even in France, music is not part of his general frame of reference.

". . . We were all insufferable—and we were right to be, for only the spirit of contradiction saves one from routinism . . ."

Movies: An individual screen for a crowd. Television: A crowd of screens for individuals.

If the art of film is that which, without mishap, can be transferred between these mediums, Cocteau was among its few practitioners. It could be argued that he was the most influential filmmaker who ever lived, and that by extension the music for his films was the right music, even though it now seems wrong.

The superimposition of music on a movie is the final process in moviemaking and can only be realized after the cutting is finished, when the film is, as they say, in the can. Then, in the recording studio, after a rehearsal, a run-through, and a preliminary taping of the composer's fresh score, the instrumentalists lay down their instruments and they, along with the director, angels, tough producers, and unmusical yes-men, raise their heads toward a screen upon which a rough cut of the film is projected simultaneously with a playback of the score. And all the spectators then decide whether the music "works," while the composer twiddles his thumbs. On the day that the music for *Beauty and the Beast* was recorded, Cocteau wrote: ". . . And now the silence, then the three white flashes which announce the image, then the image and the wonder of that synchronization which is not a synchronization, since Auric avoids it, at my request, and since it must not occur save by the grace of God . . ."

Here is the precise reverse of the method used in Hollywood, where soundtracks of, say, Aaron Copland (the American who most mirrors France's Auric in that he has composed our most distinguished movie music) must coincide to the split second with the image *before a single note is scored.*

". . . This new universe disturbs and enthralls me. I had composed my own music without realizing it, and the waves of sound from the orchestra contradict that music. Gradually Auric's score contradicts that discomfort. My music gives way to his. This music weds the film, impregnates it, exalts it, completes it . . ."

Yet Auric himself once told me that in scoring *The Blood of a Poet* he produced what is commonly known as love music for love scenes, game music for game scenes, funeral music for funeral scenes. Cocteau had the bright idea of replacing the love music with the funeral, game music with love, funeral with game. And it worked—like prosciutto and melon. Since music's power lies in an absence of literary significance, and since this power dominates all mediums it touches, any music may persuasively accompany any image or story, while inevitably dictating the *tone* of the joint effort. Music's hidden force can rescue a mediocre scene, or ruin an excellent one. As to which method, Coctelian freedom or Californian trammeling, is better, who can judge? If music can wreck the best-laid schemes, *Of Mice and Men* today is best remembered for Copland's poignantly cohering sounds, while *Beauty and the Beast*, at least to one hearer, is hampered by the insistent Heavenly Voices intruding on each frame like treacle on rubies. If I was entranced thirty-five years ago by the mixture of media, now the film and its music have both dated, one well and one badly, while *The Blood of a Poet* remains the greatest wedding on film of film and music.

Although the Parisian musical aesthetic of the 1920s—skimming away Teutonic fat and keeping "deep meaning" to a minimum—

infiltrated the United States, initially through Copland, and flourished for two decades, literary influence, specifically Cocteau's, on major figures of the next generations (with the possible exception of Paul Goodman) has been nil. It is of course through movies that Cocteau has changed forever the world's outlook, despite his name's being a cipher to American youth. With this in mind, see what the American composer, Elliott Carter (b. 1908), who, although Boulanger-educated and a Proustophile, is hardly a *prince frivole* (indeed, his working system grazes the Germanic), has to say about his own First String Quartet, written in 1950:

> . . . The general plan was suggested by Jean Cocteau's film *Le Sang d'un poète*, in which the entire dream-like action is framed by an interrupted slow-motion shot of a tall brick chimney in an empty lot being dynamited. Just as the chimney begins to fall apart, the shot is broken off and the entire movie follows, after which the shot is resumed at the point it left off, showing its disintegration in mid-air, and closing the film with its collapse on the ground. A similar interrupted continuity is employed in this quartet's starting with a cadenza for cello alone that is continued by the first violin alone at the very end. On one level, I interpret Cocteau's idea (and my own) as establishing the difference between external time (measured by the falling chimney, or the cadenza) and internal dream time (the main body of the work)—the dream time lasting but a moment of external time, but from the dreamer's point of view a long stretch. In the *First Quartet*, the opening cadenza also acts as an introduction to the rest, and when it reappears at the end, it forms the last variation in a set of variations. Not only is the plan like that of many "circular" works of modern literature, but . . .

Note that no word is said of the music—of Auric's original music—in *The Blood of a Poet*. Cocteau's influence on Carter has been visual, not aural. Obviously the quartet could never replace Auric's score, which was an embellishment of the film, for that would be like coincidental readings of Euripides' *Hippolytus* and Racine's *Phèdre*.

As with *The Blood of a Poet*, so with at least one ballet: regulate *"le synchronisme accidentale."* Proceeding on the principle that any music will fit logically with any visual, while dictating the tone—indeed, altering the very sense—of the visual, he brought to fruition a venture in which his co-workers' intentions were

Jean Cocteau. *Georges Auric*, 1921. Illustration from *Dessins*, 1924

turned inside out. In 1946 the dancers for *The Young Man and Death* were rehearsed using jazz rhythms. When the choreography was complete, it was found to last seventeen minutes, and some "real" music of that length was needed. The overture to *The Magic Flute* being prohibitively expensive, Bach's *Passacaglia* was substituted on opening night. Immediately the seventeen-minute *Passacaglia* came to sound inevitable.

What Roland Petit had permitted for *The Young Man* was vetoed four years later by Lifar for *Phèdre*. Cocteau's "chance synchronization" might have provided a more amusing choreography than Lifar's breast-beaten notions, though even Garbo (whom Cocteau originally sought for the role) could not have overshadowed the mature Toumanova, who, garbed in Cocteau's thirty-foot-wide crimson shoulder pads, paced the stage like a nineteenth-century tragedienne trapped inside a puma. And Georges Auric's score is his most "significant," outside the movies.

Did Cocteau know about music technically? Auric claims that he could pick out any tune with one finger, provided the tune was in F major.

My first week in Paris, spring of 1949, I saw a newsreel of him waving at the camera, then turning his back and blending into the horizon. A voice-over said, "Cocteau renounces public life." Puzzled by the image of a man in the act of not being a celebrity, I had yet to read his myriad denials of fame, his upcoming *Diary of an Unknown Man*, which restates: "Public life disguises and protects my secret creative life . . . To be up-to-date is to be quickly out-of-date . . . The poet must remain invisible. Etc. . . ." I could never swallow these contradictions of fact, not recognizing that they were precisely what made Cocteau Cocteau.

"A dreamer is always a bad poet," he wrote in 1921, and: *"Pelléas* is another example of music to be listened to with one's face in one's hands. All music to be listened to through the hands is suspect." Forty years later, in 1962, he did manage the direction, sets, and costumes for a production of *Pelléas and*

Mélisande, yet he always preferred Maeterlinck's play to music.

At a rehearsal of *Parade* Ravel told Cocteau that he did not understand music that was not "bathed in any sonorous fluid." Cocteau adopted an anti-Ravel stance in the early days of *Les Six*, but conciliated in 1930.

What Ravel and Debussy thought of Cocteau's *oeuvre*, if they knew it, is unrecorded. Satie was their link with him. I need scarcely repeat Satie's *mot*, "Ravel refuses the Legion of Honor but all of his music accepts it," nor Cocteau's rejoinder, "It's not enough to refuse, one must not have deserved it."

Marie-Laure offered her ballroom in December of 1932 for *le tout Paris* to attend a preview of two new works by refugee Kurt Weill: *Der Jasager*, and "the Paris version" of *Mahagonny*, conducted by Maurice Abravanel and featuring Weill's wife, Lotte Lenya. Six months later *The Seven Deadly Sins* was performed in Paris, after which Weill faded from fashion, except with Cocteau. The two plotted an opera about *Faust*, of which nothing remains but a couple of pages of music and thirteen letters from the poet, possibly because Weill felt he could never compete with his mentor Busoni's *Doktor Faustus*, or because Cocteau momentarily sensed that the transposition of romantic legends, like that of Greek myths, inevitably lacks the power of the original—although he went on to film *The Eternal Return* and *Orpheus*. I did hear Cocteau describe, many years later, his mini-Faust: "The doddering doctor sells his soul to the devil, becomes a handsome young man, presents himself to Marguerite, who merely says, 'I'm sorry, sir, but I prefer older men.'"

One remnant remains of the Weill-Cocteau friendship. Lenya recalled: "Kurt and I were invited to dine at Cocteau's one evening [in 1933]. Cocteau tried to speak a few sentences in German. Kurt expressed surprise, and asked Cocteau if he really spoke German. Cocteau answered, 'Yes—all nouns!' He then excused himself, went into another room, returned a few minutes later with a sheet of paper. On it were the first lines of *Es regnet* [It's raining]. Kurt encouraged him to finish the poem, which Cocteau eventually did. Kurt corrected some of the grammar-school errors and set it to music." The resulting song is not vintage Weill, nor is the text more than a miniature rehash of *The Human Voice*.

His only other musical intercourse with a German was still less fruitful, if more ambitious. Paul Hindemith wanted Cocteau to write him a libretto. In 1952 the poet was planning the decoration of the Villefranche chapel of Saint-Pierre, and was rereading the Apocalypse and the Gospel of Saint John. From this he drew his *Sept dialogues avec le seigneur inconnu qui est en nous (Seven Dialogues with the Unknown Lord Who Is Within Us)*, which, in turn, he adapted as an opera text of high seriousness, finishing it on September 5. Hindemith, whose musical style had never been known for its wit, had nonetheless thought of Cocteau as a humorist, and was counting on a comic libretto. Thus the poet was frustrated until a decade later, when young Yves Claoué (son of the noted "esthetic surgeon" who reshaped the nose of Juliette Greco) took the book, rebaptized *Patmos*, and made it into an opera that was premiered in the chapel of Versailles, whose sainted arches presumably shook at the mention of the great whore of Babylon who figures in the work.

This was not the first of Cocteau's musical texts to go a-begging. With Radiguet in 1920 he had prepared a libretto on *Paul et Virginie* for Satie, who spoke warmly of the music he was composing for it, although no one ever saw the score. After Satie's death Cocteau proposed the book to Poulenc, who extracted one poem by Radiguet, then passed it on to Sauguet, who extracted a *"Chanson de marin"* ("Sailor's Song"), then gave it to Nicolas Nabokov, who gave it to Valentine Hugo, who lost it.

No song settings of Cocteau's verse are stunningly worthwhile, not even those *Cocardes (Cockades)* that inspired in 1919 the young Poulenc, our century's greatest song writer. I'm not sure why. The reason has nothing to do with whether the words were expressly made to be set (as with Weill) or already existed when the composer came upon them (as with Poulenc). The libretto for the opera *Antigone* was confected for Honegger, while that of *La Voix humaine (The Human Voice)* existed in its final shape thirty-five years before Poulenc musicalized it, and both works are surely stunningly worthwhile. The best songs on Cocteau's words are the most vulgar. Listen to Poulenc's 1918 pop ditty, *"Toréador,"* if you can find it—it is seldom listed among his works; or to *"Mes soeurs, n'aimez pas les marins"* ("Sisters, Don't Fall in Love with Sailors"), with music by (I think) Paul Fort, a melancholy *scena* recorded by the *diseuse* Marianne Oswald around 1940, and which I have never come across again in any form.

Most of *Les Six* wrote Cocteau songs while very young, not later. For the record, one of my own first good songs, written at twenty in 1944, was on this quatrain called *"De Don Juan"*:

> *En Espagne on orne les rues*
> *Avec les loges d'opéra*
> *Quelle est cette belle inconnue?*
> *C'est la mort, Don Juan l'aura.*

If any composer is today searching for appropriate verse of Cocteau, let him look at the hitherto unpublished love lyrics in Jean Marais's autobiography, *Histoires de ma vie (Stories of my Life)*. They are of great truth and beauty.

There are as many Cocteaus as there are biographers of him. In our country he has now grown remote, but in the late 1960s he was subject to an American rush: Robert Phelps, Francis Steegmuller, Stephen Koch, Frederick Brown, Paul Horgan, Elizabeth Sprigge, all had their say, short or long, and each presented a different character. As I remarked of Satie—one must earn the right to disapprove—so with Cocteau, and the hostility or veneration of certain portrayals seems at times no less lazy than adroit.

Not that my own scattered notes have sprung from discipline, for I have not a scholarly bent. As cordially as possible I have collected a garland of special responses to the musical side of the poet who, more than most jacks-of-all-trades, combined the sublimely right with the unutterably trashy. If he didn't "know" anything about music, he was a shrewd layman who somehow belonged to the world of sound—*il appartenait à l'univers orphique*, said Sauguet. And if—like a song composer (a Schubert

or a Fauré) for whom poetry is a means to an end—Cocteau used music as a cloak, a source, a detachable skin, a gloss, who dares say he used it wrongly?

He didn't pretend to know more than he knew, didn't talk music in musicians' jargon, and thank God for that. But he did use musical references. (On the first day's rushes of *Beauty and the Beast* he wrote: ". . . Faults don't matter, they afford a certain relief. It was like *looking* at Mozart's music, in which the slightest detail, any four notes, can be isolated and whose movement *as a whole* is so admirable.") And he did put to wondrous use the "accidental synchronizing" that I, as a composer, find more sensible than the fussy solderings of "musical" filmmakers with a dangerous little learning who feel that music has literal meaning. (On the last day's rushes: ". . . Today is the day for the music. I have refused to hear what Auric has composed, wanting to receive the shock of it without preparation. A long habit of working together gives me complete confidence in him . . .")

His ideas for musical subjects inevitably stemmed from those of other people, such as Shakespeare and Sophocles, just as Shakespeare stems from Sophocles and Sophocles from Homer and Homer from . . . it works both ways. If Camus's *Malentendu* seems too close for comfort to Cocteau's *Pauvre Matelot* (a gloomy tale culled, so he says, from the *faits divers*), who will disagree with Gide's defense of *his* culling the *faits divers*: "I cannot understand how the merit of a work of art can be diminished through its being based on reality"?

Reality, on his best days, was transmuted by Jean Cocteau into a permanent and contagious magic that his musical collaborators occasionally captured and communicated intact to a world of listeners.

< Jean Cocteau. *Francis Poulenc*, 1922. Illustration from *Dessins*, 1924

A Musical Chronology

In 1908 a certain Tiarko Richepin and one Jacques Renaud composed songs on Jean's poetry—before Jean was Jean—and these were apparently sung at the celebrated launching of Cocteau by the tragedian de Max at the Théâtre Femina that year. In 1972 the posthumous ballet, *Le Fils de l'air (The Son of the Air)*, with music by the youngish German, Hans Werner Henze, was finally mounted in Brussels. The vast half-century between these events is accurately surveyed in Milorad's essay, "*Avec les musiciens*," in an otherwise useful book of the same title (articles on the musical Cocteau by Markevitch, Auric, Babilée, and others) published in 1978 by Gallimard in the ongoing series, *Cahiers de Jean Cocteau* (available in French only). Beyond this, does it go without saying that Cocteau bibliographies can be had for the asking? No amount of searching through the stacks of Manhattan libraries has turned up a general catalog, even slightly *raisonné*, let alone a specialized listing of musical collaborations. Thus with the help of my friend, James Holmes, I have compiled the following categories. Omitted are many a stillborn project, and many a lesser song.

BALLETS AND CHOREOGRAPHED SPECTACLES (No words)

1912   *Le Dieu bleu (The Blue God)* (Ballets Russes)
Music: Reynaldo Hahn
Choreography: Michel Fokine
Decor and costumes: Léon Bakst
First performance: Théâtre du Châtelet, Paris,
May 13, 1912
Principals: Nijinsky, Karsavina

1914   *David* (Unrealized ballet, portions of scenario later incorporated into *Parade*; Cocteau unsuccessfully sought a score from Stravinsky.)

1915   *Le Songe d'une nuit d'été (A Midsummer Night's Dream)* (Cirque Médrano. Unrealized project.)
Music: Erik Satie, with "interpolations" by Florence

Schmitt, Maurice Ravel, Igor Stravinsky, and Edgar
Varèse; Satie's *Cinq Grimaces* only music composed
Director: Firmin Gémier
Sets and costumes by Albert Gleizes exist
Principals: Fratellini Brothers as Bottom, Flute, Starve-
ling

1917 *Parade* (Ballets Russes)
Music: Erik Satie
Choreographer: Léonide Massine
Curtain, decor, and costumes: Pablo Picasso
First performance: Théâtre du Châtelet, Paris,
May 18, 1917
Principals: Zverev, Chabelska, Lopoukhova
Program manifesto: Guillaume Apollinaire

1920 *Le Boeuf sur le toit (The Ox on the Roof)* (Spectacles-
Concerts: Etienne de Beaumont)
Music: Darius Milhaud
Realization: Cocteau
Decor and costumes: Guy-Pierre Fauconnet, compiled
by Raoul Dufy
First performance: Théâtre de Comédie des Champs-
Elysées, February 21, 1920

1924 *Le Train bleu (The Blue Train)* (Ballets Russes)—
Opérette dansée
Music: Darius Milhaud
Choreography: Bronislava Nijinska
Decor: Henri Laurens, Curtain: Picasso
First performance: Théâtre des Champs-Elysées,
June 13, 1924
Principal: Dolin

1946 *Le Jeune Homme et la mort (The Young Man and Death)*
Music: J. S. Bach's *Passacaglia*
Choreographer: Roland Petit
Decor: Karinska
Costumes: Christian Bérard
First performance: Théâtre des Champs-Elysées,
June 1946
Principal: Jean Babilée

1950   *Phèdre* (Opera, Paris)
         Music: Georges Auric
         Choreography: Serge Lifar
         Decor, costumes, and scenario: Cocteau
         First performance: Paris Opéra, June 14, 1950
         Principals: Tamara Toumanova and Lifar

1953   *La Dame à la licorne (The Lady and the Unicorn)*
         Music: Sixteenth-century works arranged by Jacques
             Chailley
         Choreographer: Heinz Rosen
         Decor and costumes: Cocteau
         First performance: Munich, 1953

1959   *Le Poète et sa muse (The Poet and His Muse)*
         Music: Gian-Carlo Menotti
         Mise-en-scène: Franco Zeffirelli
         Decor, costumes, and scenario: Cocteau
         First performance: Spoleto, Italy, July 1959

1962   *Le Fils de l'air (ou l'Enfant changé en jeune homme)*
         (The Son of the Air, or The Child Became a Young
         Man). This ballet scenario, elaborately planned by
         Cocteau in 1962, was posthumously mounted only a
         decade later.
         Music: Hans Werner Henze
         Choreography: Béjart (who took great liberties with
             the book)
         Sets and costumes (supplied by Dermit): Cocteau
         First performance: Brussels, 1972

(In 1957 the Paris Opera gave a balletic version of *Le Bel indifférent (The Handsome Hunk)*, but without the intervention of
the author. Other than Lifar, who choreographed, the collaborators were not in the familiar Cocteau circle. Music was by the
conductor, Richard Blaireau; sets and costumes by the painter
Félix Labisse.)

OTHER STAGE WORKS WITH MUSICAL BASIS (With words)

OPERA:
   Le Gendarme incompris (The Misunderstood Policeman)

(1921). Libretto by Cocteau and Raymond Radiguet. Music by Francis Poulenc. First performance: Théâtre des Mathurins, May 1921. Comic opera in one act. An incorporated text of Mallarmé is proclaimed by a stock-comic gendarme in the stock-comic accent, rendering the text incomprehensible. Poulenc withdrew the music (it appears in none of his catalogs), although Milhaud claimed that "Poulenc wrote music so appetizing that I've always been sorry he refused to have it played again."

Antigone (1923). Libretto is the 1922 play of Cocteau, abridged "like a telegram," and musicalized with false accentuations by Honegger. For the original play Honegger had composed "a little score for harp and oboe."

Le Pauvre Matelot (The Poor Sailor) (1927). Music by Milhaud. A *"complainte"* in three brief acts. The text, based on a "news item" about a Roumanian crime, was created by Cocteau in Lavandou in 1922 and adapted to a French landscape. Originally intended for Auric, it was eventually used by Milhaud five years later. Much of the score is based on French sailor chanteys.

La Voix humaine (The Human Voice) (1958). Music by Poulenc. The libretto is the 1929 monologue for Berthe Bovy. Francis Poulenc had hoped for Callas in the role, which was eventually created, to great effect, by Denise Duval at the Opéra Comique.

NONOPERATIC STAGE WORKS (With words)

Les Mariés de la Tour Eiffel (The Wedding on the Eiffel Tower) (1921). Libretto and production conceived by Cocteau. First performed at the Théâtre des Champs-Elysées, June 18, 1921. Action is mimed, and the scene described by two actors with megaphones. Text resembles (or rather, influenced) the dadaistic forays in the 1960s of Frank O'Hara and Kenneth Koch. Music by all of *Les Six*, except Durey. Dance by the Swedish Ballet, Rolf de Maré, producer.

Oedipus Rex (1927). Libretto in French by Cocteau, translated (poorly) and in part by J. Danielou into Latin. Music by Stravinsky. Premiered by the Ballets Russes for Diaghilev on May 30 at the Théâtre Sarah-Bernhardt.

PLAYS EMPLOYING INCIDENTAL MUSIC

La Patience de Pénélope (The Patience of Penelope), written probably in 1910 with Reynaldo Hahn. Little remains of this *mensonge en un acte* except for a few poems by Cocteau. The prose was by one André Paysan.

Renaud et Armide. For the 1962 reprise of this play Poulenc composed what he termed *"quelques pets,"* and it was mounted in Baalbek with sets by Edouard Dermit.

Roméo et Juliette (Desormières)

L'Aigle à deux têtes (The Eagle with Two Heads) (Auric)

Oedipe-Roi (Oedipus the King) (Maurice Thiriet)

Les Chevaliers de la table ronde (The Knights of the Round Table) (Purcell)

SONGS AND CONCERT MUSIC WITH TEXTS BY COCTEAU

1918 *Toréador (Chanson hispano-italienne)*, voice and piano,
–32 Poulenc

1919 *Huit poèmes de Jean Cocteau*, voice and piano, Auric
Cocardes (Cockades), three poems for voice and piano, Francis Poulenc

1920 *Le Crabe (The Crab)*, from a set of three songs, Satie
Le Printemps au fond de la mer (Springtime at the Bottom of the Sea), cantata for soprano with wind instruments, Louis Durey
Trois poèmes de Jean Cocteau, voice and piano, Milhaud

1927 *Six poèmes de Jean Cocteau*, voice and piano, Honegger
Pièce de circonstance, song for Jane Barthori, Milhaud

1930 *Cantate*, for soprano, male chorus, and orchestra, Igor Markevitch

1954 Monologue from *Les Chevaliers de la table ronde*, trans-
–55 lated by Paul Goodman and included in *The Poets Requiem*, for soprano, chorus, and orchestra, Ned Rorem

1956 *Chat (Cat)*, Milhaud

1961 *La Dame de Monte Carlo (The Lady from Monte Carlo)*, monologue for voice and orchestra. Poulenc's last work (except for two woodwind sonatas)

MOVIES USING MUSIC

Le Sang d'un poète (The Blood of a Poet), Auric
L'Eternel Retour (The Eternal Return), Auric
La Belle et la bête (Beauty and the Beast), Auric
L'Aigle à deux têtes, Auric
Ruy Blas, Auric
Les Parents terribles (The Storm Within), Auric
Orphée (Orpheus), Auric-Gluck
Les Enfants terribles (The Holy Terrors), Bach-Vivaldi
Le Testament d'Orphée (The Testament of Orpheus)
   No music. Sound is credited.
La Voix humaine (The Human Voice), Rossellini's film with
   Anna Magnani, and sets by Bérard. Music by (I think)
   Rossellini's brother.

(In the late 1970s Antonioni made a version of *L'Aigle à deux têtes* which may have had music.)

Have I forgotten to mention that in 1920 Georges Auric composed a piano solo, for acrobats, called *Adieu New York (Farewell, New York)* on the urging of Cocteau? Or that I myself wrote the incidental music to Auden's translation of *The Knights of the Round Table*, directed by Herbert Machiz in 1967? Undoubtedly, endless numbers of scores will continue to turn up, and others will be written during the various revivals of Cocteau's plays and poems.

CHAMBER MUSIC PROGRAM
USING ONLY VOICE AND PIANO(S)

Parade (four-hand version), piano	Satie
Cocardes (song cycle), voice and piano	Poulenc
Quatre Petites Mélodies (Four Little Melodies)	
(Lamartine, Cocteau, Radiguet, Anon.)	Satie
La Dame de Monte Carlo (drame lyrique)	Poulenc
Toréador (short song)	Poulenc
Le Boeuf sur le toit	
(four-hand, or for two pianos)	Milhaud

Intermission

La Voix humaine (soprano and piano)	Poulenc

Le Sang d'un poète (Jean Cocteau, Lee Miller), 1930

The Mask in the Mirror:

 The Movies of Jean Cocteau

Stephen Harvey

NINETEEN EIGHTY-THREE marked the twentieth anniversary of the death of Jean Cocteau, a milestone commemorated in Paris by a predictable boomlet of homages to his fifty years' hard labor in eight or nine of the seven lively arts. Exhibits of his sketches and scribblings sprouted promiscuously, and Jean Marais, still his most ardent disciple, mounted a theatrical collage of his sayings and writings. And naturally, once more unreeled for reappraisal were Cocteau's contributions to what he, with his patented Grecophilia, was wont to call "The Tenth Muse." Most of the subsequent tributes in the daily and weekly press were filled with a bland reverence—probably the one critical attitude Cocteau was spared during his lifetime. Where Cocteau's movies were concerned, one thing had not changed: those French with a passion for cultural codification still did not know quite what to make of them. It was easy enough to admire *Le Sang d'un poète (The Blood of a Poet)*, *Orphée (Orpheus)*, and the rest—not without a touch of condescension, now that what had once seemed so startling in their language and imagery had inevitably become nostalgic and picturesque. That these films—a half dozen actually directed by Cocteau, a like number for which he only worked on the scripts—comprise one of the most vivid chapters in Cocteau's lifework is beyond any doubt. Whether they really count for much in the wider context of nearly a century of movie history is another and more ambiguous matter.

To diehard aesthetes for whom movies in the mainstream are by definition a trifle vulgar, this is a moot point. For them, the movies were briefly exalted because an artist like Cocteau occasionally made use of them to explore his particular vision in an unfamiliar form. (The obverse of that lofty perspective is the idea that movies sullied his artistic purity with their crass insistence on star power, tawdry notions of glamor, and more or less coherent modes of storytelling.) Those few remaining diehards who view the screen as a retarded stepchild of the theater are grateful only because the movies have preserved a few of his most celebrated stage pieces. And inveterate cinephiles are baffled because Cocteau treated the movies as an avocation rather than a life-long metier; they can't understand why anyone would resort to print or to inert images when the sensuous possibilities of the movie camera were there ready to be explored. Even the most bewitched of them can't agree on precisely *which* Cocteau film should be embraced for the ages. Third-generation avant-gardists pounce on *Le Sang d'un poète* as the pure essence of his idiosyncratic genius, of which the later, more conventionally structured movies were but a pale reflection. (And they're talking about *Orphée*—as far as they're concerned, movies on the order of *L'Aigle à deux têtes (The Eagle with Two Heads)* aren't even worth discussing.) Others with a more populist taste find *Le Sang d'un poète* precious and dilettantish; their Cocteau is the decadent Mother Goose who, in the prologue to *La Belle et la bête (Beauty and the Beast)* beseeched his audience to "let me say to you those four magic words . . . Once Upon a Time!" Finally, there are those believers in the *politique des vedettes* who prize Cocteau as male midwife to the stars, a kind of Gallic George Cukor. Their most treasured images are not his crackpot-

Odalisque plaster casts and crumpled drapery, but closeups of Maria Casarès as the Daughter of Darkness and Jean Marais as the fallen angel. Only God could have created Marais, perhaps, but it was Cocteau who sculpted his pedestal.

Cocteau really had himself to blame for this fragmented perspective where his film legacy was concerned. His sensibility permeates all of his movies with an amazing consistency, but the impulses behind his sporadic descents into the cinema were various in the extreme, as the movies themselves testify. Cocteau was by turns an intransigent individualist who was not above accommodating the tastes of *le tout Paris*, and a rarefied poet who wooed the masses with fractured fairy tales and primordial legends. At the time of *Le Sang d'un poète*, Cocteau claimed that film attracted him as a new vehicle for intense self-expression, a kind of "ink made out of light." Ten years later, in an interview subsequently quoted in Francis Steegmuller's biography, Cocteau said, "I made *L'Eternel Retour (The Eternal Return)* . . . to build a bridge that would bring together film connoisseurs and the public at large." When the interviewer asked if Cocteau was dismayed by the film's wide popularity, he proclaimed to the contrary, he was proud of it. Besides, he might well have added, his protégé Marais wanted film stardom in the worst way, and this was the project guaranteed to achieve it.

If Cocteau was something of a chameleon (and rather gloried in that fact), the one thing he was not was a rebel impatiently prodding the French cinema to venture into alien terrain. In the thirty-year trajectory of his screen career, nothing he did was entirely without precedent—in fact, he proved amazingly adroit at sensing changes in the cultural temperature, and shaping his films to accommodate them. The startling imagery of *Le Sang d'un poète* jolted many at its public premiere in 1932, but the fact of its existence could scarcely have astonished anyone in the avant-garde. Such conscious experiments in using film as an extension of poetry and the plastic arts had been conducted throughout the 1920s by, among others, Man Ray, Léger, and Germaine Dulac. Some of the film's sensation was surely blunted by the advent, three years earlier, of Buñuel and Dali's *Un Chien andalou*, commissioned, like the Cocteau film, by the

Le Sang d'un poète (Enrique Rivero), 1930

Le Sang d'un poète, 1930

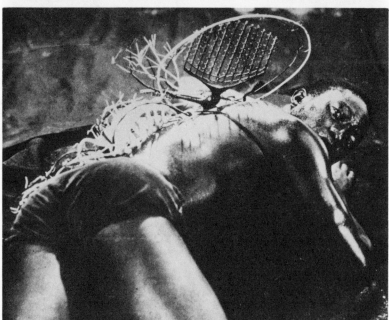

Le Sang d'un poète, 1930

Vicomte de Noailles. *Le Sang d'un poète* may have been Sur-
real in a general sense, but it wasn't really Surrealist; the members of that narrow fraternity found Cocteau too much the *chic
arriviste* to be one of them. And if the fiercest admirers of *Le
Sang d'un poète* decried Cocteau's shift to more prosaic feature
films in the 1940s, others might well have wondered what took
him so long. Jean Renoir and René Clair had both dabbled in
playful nonnarrative forms in the 1920s, and abandoned them
even before sound came to the screen. By the early 1930s, the
moment for recherché items like *Le Sang d'un poète* was waning,
in any case. Economic conditions made such private patrons as
de Noailles increasingly wary; the political climate gradually
persuaded much of Parisian bohemia that there were more immediate and urgent concerns than goosing the bourgeoisie.

Cocteau wrote his first screenplay in 1940, the year France
was occupied and a crucial year of decision for members of the
French film industry. Directors such as Renoir, Clair, Julien
Duvivier, and Jacques Feyder chose or were compelled to emi-
grate for the duration of the war, as did a considerable propor-
tion of the French screen's roster of stars—Jean Gabin, Louis
Jouvet, Michèle Morgan, Victor Francen, Marcel Dalio. Perverse-
ly, the French cinema flourished during the Occupation; it
was the one affordable diversion left to the populace at large,
made even more attractive after the ban on American movies
went into effect. The link between the boulevards and the studios
had always been closer, geographically and otherwise, than that
between Broadway and Hollywood, and Cocteau was not the
only distinguished playwright to turn to the movies at this point;
Giraudoux and Anouilh both wrote for the screen under the
Occupation. Yet neither was as prolific as Cocteau, who wrote
four screenplays during this period.

Cocteau was hardly the sort of artist to be troubled by the fact
that any audible reverberations of the political realities of the
times were strictly *verboten*. And the movies he wrote floated
through that same tenebrous never-never land in which most of
the films made in France during the war years were situated. He
began with *La Comédie du bonheur (Comedy of Happiness)*,
directed by Marcel L'Herbier, another regenerate avant-gardist,

and shot mainly in Rome. The film concerns a benign madman (Michel Simon) who hires a troupe of actors to bring illusion and romance to the morbid inhabitants of a second-rate pension; it concludes with an accelerated chase through the Futuristic decor of a television station, in the style of the departed René Clair. Next came Serge de Poligny's *Le Baron fantôme (The Phantom Baron)*, one of a series of wartime nineteenth-century Gothics about misalliances among the ruins of an even more distant seigneurial age. Its heroine is named Elfy, which should give some idea of its tone; she was played by Odette Joyeux, a Martha Scott look-alike who specialized in this sort of role. Toward the end of the film Cocteau himself made a cameo appearance as the title character, mummified for decades in a hidden cul-de-sac of his decrepit castle.

The third and most celebrated of the wartime scripts, and the first for which Cocteau created both story and dialogue, was Jean Delannoy's *L'Eternel Retour*, in which Tristan and Isolde are updated to Patrice (Marais) and Nathalie (Madeleine Sologne) in a "contemporary" setting—if such could be said about a France without a uniformed German in sight. In this version of the Celtic legend, it is immediately apparent that the stream-lined lovers were destined for each other, because nobody else in the world could be as blond as they are. The Parisian bobby-soxers went mad for the film, but after the war more captious viewers in England and the States saw suspiciously Aryan under-tones to it all. Certainly the seductive inevitability of death was a theme that had captivated Cocteau long before *L'Eternel Retour*. It is also quite probable that the film would not have been made at all had it not been for the enormous success the previous year of the Carné-Prevert *Les Visiteurs du soir (The Night Visitors)*, with its own pair of ill-starred *amoureux* whose hearts continue to beat after their bodies have been transmuted into stone.

Yet Cocteau wrote his most distinguished screenplay for the relatively obscure *Les Dames du Bois de Boulogne (The Ladies of the Bois de Boulogne)*, an unlikely collaboration with the ascetic director Robert Bresson, which was released soon after the war. Framed though it is with Bresson's withering objectivity, the world of *Les Dames du Bois de Boulogne* is emphatically Cocteau's—the claustrophobic luxe of an *haut-monde* Paris. The story focuses on the cosmopolitan Hélène, played by Maria Casarès; spurned by her equally well-born lover, she engineers a liaison for him with a floozy paid to masquerade as a provincial bourgeoise. As in most of Cocteau's later films, passion here is a hypothetical conceit; if these characters are scorched by any emotion, it's the dry ice of egotism. The images that endure are of Casarès, stalking the *seizième arrondissement* in her somber Schiaparelli glad rags like a vengeful emissary from the most soigné corner of Hell. Bresson found the experience of bucking the self-protective temperaments of his stars such a trial that he vowed henceforth to use only nonprofessional actors in his films. Cocteau, however, was clearly dazzled by Casarès; a few years later they had a rendezvous for *Orphée*, in which her opaque, embittered allure acquired even more explicitly infernal shadings.

La Belle et la bête, released the year after the end of the war, epitomized what the New Wave critics-turned-filmmakers were later, and derisively, to call the "tradition of quality"—movies with a literary pedigree, shot on aquarium-lit soundstages, with star personalities declaiming meticulously articulate set speeches. Yet by the force and consistency of his imagination, Cocteau managed at the same time to rise above this category; thanks to a directorial eye that was anything but literal, if obviously literary, he was largely spared the wrath of the New Wave in years to come. *Ruy Blas*, a costume melodrama Cocteau adapted from Victor Hugo and entrusted to the journeyman director Pierre Billon, was not nearly as transcendent. Its principal attractions were its deoxygenated baroque decors and the opportunity it gave Marais to essay the dual role of noble highwayman and humble student. The film thrilled the fans of Marais and his co-star Danielle Darrieux and riled the Victor Hugo estate, which resented Cocteau's alterations of the sacred text; *Ruy Blas* bored just about everybody else.

With *L'Aigle à deux têtes (The Eagle with Two Heads)*, *Les Parents terribles*, and *Orphée*, Cocteau belatedly followed a route traveled back in the 1930s by Marcel Pagnol and Sacha Guitry—to give permanence to his texts for the stage by translat-

La Belle et la bête (Jean Marais), 1946

La Belle et la bête (Josette Day), 1946

ing them to the screen. In tone and subject, *Les Parents terribles* (English film title: *The Storm Within*) is about as far removed as possible from the work of the prolific boulevardier Guitry, but Cocteau's filmmaking strategy was virtually identical. He confined all action to the two interior sets specified in the playscript, which was performed mainly by the actors responsible for its stage triumph—Marais, of course, plus the two character actresses most beloved by Cocteau, Gabrielle Dorziat as Marais's sage aunt, and Yvonne de Bray as his suffocating, Pekingese-faced mother. If *Les Parents terribles* was a triumph of reactionary film technique, *Orphée* looked like the last word in 1950s contemporaneity, even though Cocteau adapted it, rather loosely, from a play dating back to the mid-1920s. All the usual Cocteau calligraphy is here—the dangerous lure of a mirror's reflection, death as a corridor in limbo. Yet *Orphée*'s cool embrace of more modern tics is just as striking. Its harsh black-and-white photography and the use of rubble-strewn wartime ruins as the netherworld between Life and Death conjured up the postwar

Italian school led by Rossellini and de Sica, then very much à la mode throughout Europe. In a sense, however, Cocteau went them all one better—*Orphée* transformed Neo-realism into the supernatural.

The making of *Les Enfants terribles (The Holy Terrors)*, from Cocteau's novel first published in 1930, was prompted in part by the success of *Les Parents*, plus Cocteau's hope that it would prove an effective film showcase for his most recent find, Edouard Dermit. (He had already appeared in *Orphée* as the punk poet who has stolen the lyric thunder of the more mature artist, Orphée-Marais.) This was Cocteau's sole miscalculation, as Dermit's Paul was utterly effaced by the somber, troubling sister Elisabeth of Nicole Stéphane. Otherwise, *Les Enfants terribles* is one Cocteau project that can truly be said to have anticipated a future current in the French screen. Its youthful central pair, rootless and spontaneous, linked both by blood and their shared morbidity, directly foreshadows the protagonists of *A Bout de souffle, Les Cousins*, and *Jules et Jim*, brought to life by a new generation of filmmakers ten years later. Much of its freshness can be attributed to Cocteau's happy choice of Jean-Pierre Melville, the New Wave's immediate precursor, as director. His ironic bravado provided a subtle counterpoint to Cocteau's dirge of predestination. Yet curiously enough, the most Cocteauesque passages—the languorous murk of Paul and Elisabeth's airtight cave—are shaped by the director's own voyeuristic eye, while the moment that seems most Melville's, an aimless afternoon spent in the melancholy of a French seashore in the off-season, was actually shot by Cocteau on a day Melville was indisposed.

The 1950s was a quiescent period for the French cinema, and Cocteau followed the example of several of his gifted contemporary filmmakers—he absented himself, grumbling. (Even the great Renoir produced only two films in France during these years.) *Le Testament d'Orphée* emerged in 1960, just when the New Wave had made cryptic self-perusal on a shoestring fashionable once more. The film was in fact largely financed on the profits from Truffaut's *Les Quatre Cents Coups (The Four Hundred Blows)*. Cocteau conceived it, perhaps too literally, as a

Les Parents terribles (Yvonne de Bray), 1948 >

Les Parents terribles (Jean Marais and Josette Day), 1948

sort of matching bookend to his first film, *Le Sang d'un poète*. This is Cocteau's most narcissistic film, in the nonerotic sense of the term. Its protagonist, Cocteau himself, ambles through the reliquary of his life's work—a tapestry over here, reincarnated figures from a past Cocteau movie there, Oedipus on one side of him, pagan boys dolled up as horses on the other. A hellish court accuses him of the capital crime of Innocence; in what is probably the most disingenuous moment in any Cocteau movie, he proudly admits that the accusation is true. He who was by then France's most lionized living man of arts and letters insists that the public at large despises and misunderstands him—only Picasso and a tot representing the Open Childlike Spirit truly appreciate him for what he is. This is Cocteau for groupies. It is ironic that his last film is one that most resists reappraisal.

If *Le Testament* was a love letter to himself, Cocteau viewed much of his earlier film work as candid self-portraiture. "Without realizing it at the time, I was depicting myself," Cocteau has said of *Le Sang d'un poète*. "I've put my entire life inside this film," he declared during an interview at the time of *Orphée*. The French film historian Claude Beylie has justly noted that these films offer us Cocteau's autograph rather than his autobiography, yet there is considerable truth in its creator's assertion about *Orphée*. Orpheus confronts a temporal fate that Cocteau clearly feared for himself—he is an aging literary anachronism in an Existentialist time. Yet as Cocteau knew perfectly well, there was something crucial missing in *Orphée*, considered as a work of self-examination. The real tragedy for a Cocteau-Orphée would be the prospect of eternity on earth with the likes of Eurydice. Even for a public as relatively sophisticated as Cocteau's, the concrete representation of his homosexuality was inadmissible. (He certainly wasn't the least bit coy about it where his personal life was concerned.) Cocteau's solution, conscious or not, was to translate homosexuality into a kind of mystical male auto-eroticism on screen, from the serpentine posturings of a seminude Enrique Rivero, the Poet in his first film, through Marais to Dermit. Is that ecstasy or exquisite anguish on Marais's face, as he presses a perfect cheekbone

Orphée (Maria Casarès, Edouard Dermit, François Périer,
and Jean Marais), 1950

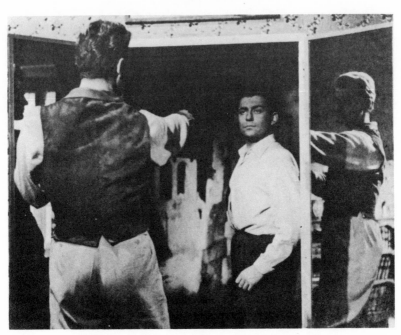

Orphée (Jean Marais and François Périer), 1950

Le Testament d'Orphée, 1960

Le Testament d'Orphée, 1960

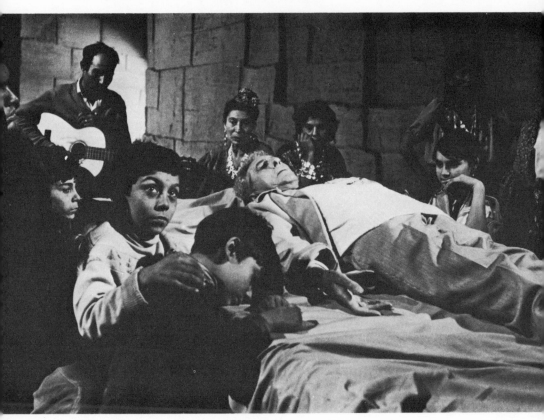

Le Testament d'Orphée, 1960

against that looking-glass that opens into the void? Probably both, since the reflection is both luscious and rather cold comfort. In *Les Enfants terribles*, Edouard Dermit's Paul does not need mirrors—in his sister, he has his own disturbing double staring back at him in the flesh.

Most of Cocteau's films speak obsessively of the consuming bonds between men and women, but since his erotic imagery is so bound up with the self—or its idealization—his celluloid love stories usually turn out to be peculiarly sexless. From *L'Eternel Retour* through *Les Enfants terribles*, chances are about even that romance will lead to death for both parties—and not such a bad thing after all, since in Cocteau's dream book, that state is a

Les Enfants terribles (Edouard Dermit and Nicole Stéphane), 1950

much more intoxicating enigma than our mere mortal existence. The sole redemption possible for the male (in *Orphée* and *Les Parents terribles)* is the devotion of a pure, sane woman. This sort of wishful thinking is clearly too hypothetical for Cocteau to bring to life. Cocteau's Good Girls are about as insubstantial as that Phantom Baron he once played, who crumbled at a touch. Marie Déa's Eurydice is a kind of Gallic June Allyson, wan stuff compared to the hypnotic glamour of the Underworld. Even the radiant Josette Day in *Les Parents terribles* seems too passive to pull Marais out of the centrifugal force of his cozy, self-devouring family. The viewer can scarcely expect to be moved by the forbearance of these women, when it is obvious that they bore Cocteau silly. The only time the attraction of opposites really stirs Cocteau is when it is pushed to unreal extremes. No wonder *La Belle et la bête* is the most compelling heterosexual romance in the Cocteau movie canon. Beauty and her Beast are not just of the opposite sex—they belong to different species.

When Cocteau represents something he cannot quite feel, the masquerade begins in earnest. Out come the trappings of archaic High Art (strains of Liebestod alternated with The-Greeks-Had-a-Word-for-It), or at the very least, haute couture. This kind of inflated flossiness reaches its peak in *L'Aigle à deux têtes*, in which a nineteenth-century Austrian monarch (Edwige Feuillère) is stalked by a murderous anarchist (Marais, of course) who is the mirror image of her late husband. Each becomes the prey of the other, they love, they die. Cocteau's explanation of the film's commercial failure was a model of unintended irony: "Our mistake, Bérard's [the movie's art director] and mine, was to be too truthful," he claimed. "The public no longer knows the first thing about queens. They hold tight to a conventional notion of what they are, where reality is the only thing that matters." Well. The truth about *L'Aigle à deux têtes* is that la Feuillère, with her cello-vibrato oratory and a coiffure embellished with rhinestone stars, bears about the same relation to Elisabeth of Austria as Norma Shearer did to Marie Antoinette. Which is not to say that *L'Aigle à deux têtes* is not satisfying, in a batty sort of way. The more synthetic the movie gets, the more its stars secrete that irresistible conviction in the power of their own talent and pulchritude. Feuillère glories in impersonating a being possessed of an imperious stare and a fragile heart, who also gets to shoot pool and bear arms, and take the best dive down a staircase since Scarlett O'Hara. Marais knows he looks great in lederhosen and an expression denoting schizoid emotions. Under Cocteau's tutelage, their sincere phoniness makes *L'Aigle à deux têtes* the essence of enjoyable kitsch.

But for art, and the "reality" Cocteau talks about, you have to look elsewhere in his filmography. As a director, he was most expressive and least evasive working in the polarities of the Baroque and the Minimalist. The difference between *L'Aigle à*

L'Aigle à deux têtes (Jean Marais and Edwige Feuillère), 1947 **>**

Les Parents terribles (Jean Marais, Jean Cocteau, Josette Day), 1948

deux têtes and *La Belle et la bête* is the contrast of fussy falseness with seamless artifice. He uses all the cinematic means he can muster to give tangible form to a spectral fable—a figure who is half King Kong, half Toto, and all man; a heroine whose tears turn into jewels; human arms as multi-directional lamps; people floating through space like creatures at the bottom of an enchanted sea. The beauty of Cocteau's movie is enriched by its creepiness. This lesson was not lost on moviemakers who evoked his visions in later years—the nightmares and looking-glasses that condense and pervert reality in Vincent Minnelli's musicals and melodramas, Ingmar Bergman's vision of Death as a grim gamester in billowing black robes.

Cocteau also saw that the ordinary human soul could be beautiful in its creepiness, and when that is his subject, his taste for symbolic froufrou evaporates. *Les Parents terribles* is both Cocteau's most hermetic movie and as complete a rendering of a fictional universe as the screen has given us. Cocteau's camera closes in on Yvonne de Bray's fetid boudoir more relentlessly than the theatergoer's eye ever could. Forcing the lens outdoors for a breath of fresh air would have violated this movie. There *is* no world outside the domestic debris of this apartment that counts to these people—that's much of their tragedy. With this work and *La Voix humaine* (filmed in Italian but intact by Roberto Rossellini, with Anna Magnani giving an audacious, terrifying performance), Cocteau makes weakness and torment paradoxically vital—these characters expend so much energy and eloquence on their way to oblivion.

Cocteau shares this talent, and much else, with America's theatrical poet of the interior, Tennessee Williams. The keening rejected mistress of *La Voix humaine* is the greatest Williams heroine he never created, and it's no accident that it took a Cocteau to adapt *A Streetcar Named Desire* for the French stage. Even Cocteau could tire of gazing into the mirror with that protective classical mask attached to his face. If the camouflage rarely dropped, his line of vision sometimes shifted outward, to the benefit of both the observer and his creations. It wasn't the blood of the poet that mattered, so much as the imagination and empathy of the artist.

A Jean Cocteau Chronology
Bernard Delvaille

1889   July 5: Clément Eugène-Jean-Maurice Cocteau is born at Maisons-Laffitte (Seine-et-Oise), France. His father, a man of independent means, was the son of a notary; his mother belonged to a family of stockbrokers.

1899   April 5: Cocteau's father commits suicide. The family takes up residence at rue La Bruyère, the home of his maternal grandfather.

1900–1905   October: Cocteau enters the sixth form at Petit Lycée Condorcet. His schoolwork is mediocre. He begins to frequent the circus, theaters, and concerts. In 1902 he moves up to the fourth form at the Grand Lycée Condorcet, which he leaves at Easter the following year. He continues his studies with private tutors, and then at the Institut Fénelon.

1906   April: His grandfather dies. Having failed the *baccalauréat* examination, Cocteau enrolls in classes with M. Dietz, with whom he boards on the rue Claude-Bernard.

1907   The family moves to 62, avenue de Malakoff. Soon Cocteau lives there alone with his mother, his sister having married and his brother having gone into business as a stockbroker. He falls in love with Madeleine Carlier, "a struggling young actress," he was to write in 1962, "whom Liane de Pougy Ghika compared to a nectarine and whose tousled hair, piled on top of her head, prefigured Brigitte Bardot's hairstyle." He gives up his studies after two more failures at the *baccalauréat*.

1908   April 4: Edouard de Max, the well-known actor, organizes a poetry reading at the Théâtre Femina, where Laurent Tailhade presents "the poems of a very young, eighteen-year-old poet, Jean Cocteau." Cocteau associates with Catulle Mendes, Anna de Noailles, Reynaldo Hahn, and becomes friends with

< Romaine Brooks. *Portrait of Jean Cocteau*, 1913. Musée National d'Art Moderne, Paris

Jean Cocteau as a school boy at Petit Lycée Condorcet, 1901–02

Maurice Rostand. A brief liaison with the actress Christiane Mancini. July 15: His first published work appears in the magazine *Je sais tout (I know everything)*. In September he travels to Venice.

1909 February: Cocteau publishes his first collection of poems, *La Lampe d'Aladin (Aladdin's Lamp)* at his own expense (Société d'Editions). He surreptitiously rents a room looking out on the gardens of the Hotel Biron, where Rilke was secretary to Rodin. May: Serge Diaghilev presents the Ballets Russes at the Théâtre du Châtelet. Cocteau founds the little magazine

Leonetto Cappielo. *de Max*. Musée d'Orsay, Paris

Jacques-Emile Blanche. *Jean Cocteau*, 1912. Musée des Beaux-Arts, Rouen

Schéhérazade with Maurice Rostand and François Bernard. He meets Diaghilev.

1910 Cocteau's poems, *Le Prince frivole (The Frivolous Prince)*, are published by Mercure de France. Cocteau continues to live with his mother at 10 rue d'Anjou. He meets Igor Stravinsky.

1911 Cocteau executes posters and drawings for Diaghilev's *Le Spectre de la Rose (The Specter of the Rose)*.

1912 Cocteau publishes the volume of poems *La Danse de Sophocle (The Dance of Sophocles)* with Mercure de France. March and April: He travels to Algeria with Lucien Daudet. May 15: Nijinsky creates *Le Dieu bleu (The Blue God)*, a ballet Cocteau had written in collaboration with Reynaldo Hahn. Cocteau corresponds with André Gide.

1913 Cocteau has *Les Vingt-sept Poèmes de Bachir-Salem (Twenty-seven Poems from Bachir-Salem)* and *Deux vivants et une morte (Two Living and One Dead)* set in type, and probably printed in an extremely limited edition. In the autumn he travels to Switzerland, where he works with Stravinsky on his ballet *David*. He completes the book *Le Potomak (The Potomac)*. November 23: His review of Marcel Proust's *Du Côté de chez Swann (Swann's Way)* appears in *Excelsior*.

1914–1916 Cocteau is excused from military service. He serves as a volunteer civilian ambulance corpsman (under German bombardment) at Reims, then in the trenches on the Belgian front at Nieuport. He visits Maurice Barrès. He writes *Le Cap du Bonne-Espérance (The Cape of Good Hope)* and *Le Discours du grand sommeil (Words on the Great Sleep)*. November: He meets the aviator Roland Garros. With Paul Iribe he founds the review *Le Mot (The Word)*. He frequents Montmartre and Montparnasse, where he meets Picasso, Braque, Derain, Juan Gris, Modigliani, Apollinaire, Max Jacob, Blaise Cendrars, Erik Satie, Kisling, and later Morand and Breton.

1917 March: Cocteau visits Rome and Naples with Diaghilev, Stravinsky, and Picasso. May 18: The premiere of *Parade* by the Ballets Russes takes place at the Théâtre du Châtelet. June 21:

Jean Cocteau at Le Piquey, 1917. Collection Edouard Dermit

Cocteau attends the only performance of *Les Mamelles de Tirésias (The Breasts of Tiresias)* by Apollinaire. September: He stays for the first time at Le Piquey on the Arcachon Basin near Bordeaux.

1918 January 15: The first recital by the *Groupe des Six* takes place at the Théâtre du Vieux-Colombier. During the spring, Cocteau, with Cendrars, revives the Editions de la Sirène (founded

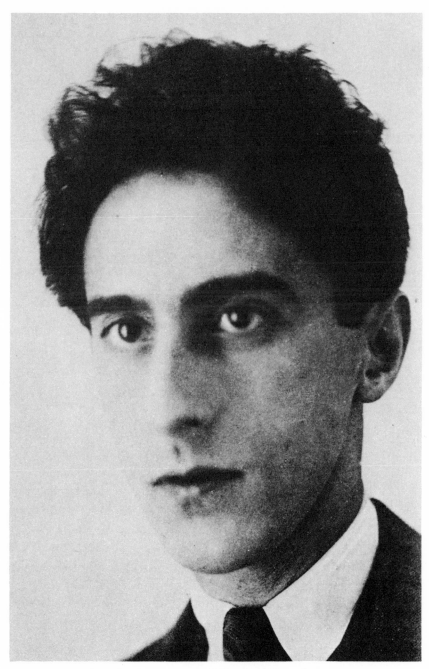

Jean Cocteau, c. 1913. Collection Edouard Dermit

a year earlier by Paul Lafitte), where he publishes seven of his books between 1918 and 1922, and where he brought Raymond Radiguet's *Le Diable au corps (Devil in the Flesh)*, only immediately to take it back and give it to the publisher Grasset. October 5: Roland Garros dies. November 5: Apollinaire dies. December: The publication of Cocteau's *Le Coq et l'Arlequin (The Cock and the Harlequin)* provokes a quarrel with Stravinsky. Cocteau's relations with the future Surrealists are also undergoing difficulties.

1919   Cocteau publishes *Le Cap de Bonne-Espérance* (which triggers an exchange of open letters with Gide in *La Nouvelle Revue Française* and *Les Ecrits Nouveaux*), the *Ode à Picasso (Ode to Picasso)*, and *Le Potomak*. He meets Radiguet.

1920   February 21: The premiere of *Le Boeuf sur le toit (The Ox on the Roof)* by the Fratellini at the Comédie des Champs-Elysées, with music by Darius Milhaud and decor by Raoul Dufy. May: Cocteau founds the review *Le Coq (The Cock)* with Radiguet. He brings out *Escales (Ports of Call)* with illustrations by André Lhote, and *Poésies 1917–1920 (Poetry 1917–1920)*. He quarrels with Tristan Tzara and Picabia.

1921   March: Cocteau stays at Carqueiranne with Radiguet. May 24: *Le Gendarme incompris (The Misunderstood Policeman)*, a musical farce by Cocteau and Radiguet, is presented at the Théâtre Michel. June 18: The Swedish Ballet presents *Les Mariés de la Tour Eiffel (The Wedding on the Eiffel Tower)* at the Théâtre des Champs-Elysées (music by Auric, Honegger, Milhaud, Poulenc, and Tailleferre). He summers at Piquey with Radiguet. *La Noce massacrée (The Massacred Wedding)* is published.

1922   January 10: The opening of the *Le Boeuf sur le toit* bar on the rue Boissy-d'Anglas, according to a note by Jean Hugo. Cocteau makes long visits to Le Lavandou and Cap Nègre with Radiguet. November 18: Marcel Proust dies. December 20: The première of *Antigone* at the Théâtre de l'Atelier is disrupted by a group of Surrealists. During this year, Cocteau is reconciled with Gide.

Giovanni Boldini. *Comte de Montesquiou*, 1897. Social archetype after whom the young Cocteau modeled himself before his conversion to the avant-garde. Musée d'Orsay, Paris

1923 May 3: Cocteau lectures at the Collège de France. His lecture is entitled *"D'un ordre considéré comme une anarchie"* ("Order Considered as Anarchy"). July to October: He is with Radiguet at Piquey. Radiguet publishes *Le Diable au corps.* Cocteau publishes *Le Grand Ecart (The Splits)*, *Plain-chant (Plainsong)*, and *Thomas l'Imposteur (Thomas the Impostor)*. December 12: Raymond Radiguet dies. Cocteau leaves Paris for Monte Carlo.

1924 January 27: Cocteau returns to Paris. June 2: *Roméo et Juliette (Romeo and Juliet)* is presented at the Théâtre de la Cigale. Cocteau is in the cast. June 20: The Ballets Russes dance *Le Train bleu (The Blue Train)*, with music by Milhaud, at the Théâtre des Champs-Elysées. July: Cocteau meets Jacques Maritain, who will exercise an important religious influence on him and bring him into association with the writers of the collection *Le Roseau d'or (The Golden Reed)*. Cocteau makes the acquaintance of Maurice Sachs. He publishes Picasso and *Poésies 1916–1923 (Poetry 1916–1923)* and drafts the preface to *Bal du Comte d'Orgel (The Ball of Count Orgel)*, Radiguet's last novel.

1925 Cocteau meets Jean Bourgoint and his sister, who serve as the models for *Les Enfants terribles (The Holy Terrors)*. February 21: An exhibition of drawings and manuscripts by Cocteau opens in Brussels. March and April: Cocteau undergoes his first detoxification treatment for opium addiction. It is followed by a stay at the Hôtel des Reservoirs in Versailles. August to October: He is at Villefranche with Christian Bérard. August 29: Cocteau is godfather at the Catholic baptism of Maurice Sachs. He makes his first *objets-poèmes*. He publishes *Cri écrit (Written Cry)*, *L'Ange Heurtebise (The Angel Heurtebise)*, *Le Mystère de Jean l'Oiseleur (The Mystery of Jean the Fowler)*, and *Prière mutilée (Disfigured Prayer)*. He begins to correspond with Jean Desbordes. He is reconciled with Stravinsky and collaborates with him on the oratorio *Oedipus Rex*.

1926 June 17: Cocteau's play, *Orphée (Orpheus)*, with the Pitoëffs, opens at the Théâtre des Arts. Cocteau publishes *La Lettre à Jacques Maritain (Letter to Jacques Maritain)*, which

< Jacques-Emile Blanche. *Les Six* (detail), 1920. Musée des Beaux-Arts, Rouen

Man Ray. *Francis Picabia*, 1922

consecrates their break. He also publishes *Maison de santé (Mental Hospital)*, and *Le Rappel à l'ordre (Call to Order)*. The Galerie Quatre-Chemins (where Maurice Sachs worked) holds an exhibition of Cocteau's *Poésie plastique*.

1927   May 30: *Oedipus Rex* opens at the Théâtre Sarah Bernhardt. Stravinsky conducts. Cocteau summers on the Riviera with Jean Desbordes. He publishes *Opéra*, and his *Le Pauvre Matelot (The Poor Sailor)*, with music by Milhaud, is performed at the Opéra-Comique. December 27: His opera *Antigone* is performed in Brussels.

1928   The Galerie Quatre Chemins exhibits *25 Dessins d'un dormeur (25 Drawings of a Sleeping Man)*. Maurice Sachs publishes *Le Mystère laïc (Laïc Mystery)* and *Le Livre blanc (The White Book)* through the gallery. *The White Book* is published without the author's or publisher's names. June: Cocteau publishes *Oedipe-Roi (Oedipus the King)* and *Roméo et Juliette*

Man Ray. *Georges Braque*, 1930 ➤

(Romeo and Juliet). December-March 1929: Cocteau undergoes new detoxification treatment at Saint-Cloud. There he meets Raymond Roussel.

1929 March: Cocteau records poems from *Opéra* for Columbia Records. March 19: A reading of *La Voix humaine (The Human Voice)* is given at the Comédie-Française. August 19: Diaghilev dies in Venice. *Les Enfants terribles* and *Une Entrevue sur la critique (A Glimpse of Criticism)* are published.

1930 February 17: The actress Berthe Bovy performs *La Voix humaine*. June 4: *Cantate* (with music by Markevitch) has its first performance at Théâtre Pigalle. During the summer, Cocteau shoots *Le Sang d'un poète (The Blood of a Poet)*, his first film, commissioned by Charles de Noailles. *Opium* is published.

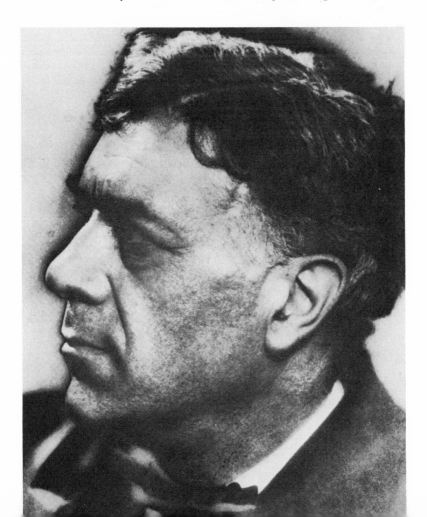

1931   Cocteau spends the summer at Toulon with Desbordes and Bérard. Stricken by typhoid, he is cared for by the Bourdets. In the fall he rents an apartment at 9, rue Vignon, Paris.

1932   January 20: the first screening of *Le Sang d'un poète* is held at the Théâtre du Vieux-Colombier. Cocteau embarks on a liaison with Natalie Paley. In August he completes his first mural (at the Bourdets). He writes *La Machine infernale (The Infernal Machine)* and publishes *Essai de critique indirecte (An Essay on Indirect Criticism)* and *Morceaux choisis (Selected Pieces).*

1933   April 30: Anna de Noailles dies. Cocteau meets Marcel Khill. In November *Le Fantôme de Marseille (The Phantom of Marseilles)* appears in *La Nouvelle Revue Française.* December: Cocteau undergoes a new detoxification treatment. He breaks with Jean Desbordes.

1934   April 10: Jouvet produces *La Machine infernale* (with sets by Bérard) at the Comédie des Champs-Elysées. Cocteau spends part of the summer in Switzerland at the home of the Noailles. September: He becomes friends with Louise de Vilmorin. Giorgio de Chirico illustrates *Mythologie (Mythology).*

1935   January–May: Cocteau's *Portraits-Souvenir (Memory Portraits)* appears in *Le Figaro.* He spends the summer at Villefranche with Khill. August: He contributes "*Retrouvons notre enfance*" ("Let Us Return to Childhood"), a series of articles, to *Paris-soir.* He publishes *60 Dessins pour les Enfants terribles (60 Drawings for The Holy Terrors).*

1936   March 28–June 17: Cocteau writes *Tour du Monde en 80 Jours (Around the World in 80 Days)* with Khill for *Paris-soir.* (They publish the account from August 1 to September 3.) *L'Ecole pour veuves (School for Widows)* is produced at the Théâtre d'ABC.

1937   March 1937–June 1939: Cocteau's collaboration at *Ce Soir*, where Louis Aragon (with whom he has reconciled) arranged for publication of his "*Articles de Paris*" ("Editorials About Paris"). A spring exhibition of drawings is held at the

Galerie Quatre Chemins. July 12: A production of *Oedipe-Roi* (the play) with Jean Marais (Cocteau has discovered Marais at an audition). September 9: Cocteau arranges the comeback of the black American boxer Al Brown, former bantam-weight champion of the world. October 14: *Les Chevaliers de la table ronde (The Knights of the Round Table)* is produced.

1938 Al Brown wins back his crown as world champion (in Paris). November 14: *Les Parents terribles (Intimate Relations)* is produced at the Théâtre des Ambassadeurs; the play is closed on December 23 by the Municipal Council of Paris.

1939 *Les Parents terribles* reopens at the Théâtre des Bouffes-Parisiens. Cocteau collaborates on dialogues for *La Comédie de bonheur (Comedy of Happiness)*, a film of Marcel L'Herbier, which is shot in 1940. He reedits the first version of *La Machine á ècrire (The Typewriter)*. Claude Mauriac begins a book on Cocteau.

1940 Cocteau settles at 36, rue de Montpensier in the Palais-Royal. February 17: The premiere of *Les Monstres sacrés (The Sacred Monsters)* is held at the Théâtre Michel. April 19: Edith Piaf appears in *Le Bel Indifférent (The Handsome Hunk)* at the Théâtre des Bouffes-Parisiens. June: Cocteau travels to Perpignan, where he is joined by Marcel Khill. In the fall he undergoes his last detoxification cure. *La Fin du Potomak (The End of Potomac)* is published. December 5: His *"Adresse aux jeunes écrivains: les territoires du l'esprit"* ("An Address to Young Writers: the Territories of the Spirit") appears in *La Gerbe*.

1941 January 2: *"A ceux qui ont écrit"* ("To Those Who Have Written") appears in *La Gerbe*. February: Cocteau records a "Spoken Preface" for *Britannicus*, a play staged by Jean Marais at the Théâtre des Bouffes-Parisiens. April 29: Raymond Rouleau presents *La Machine à écrire* at the Théâtre des Arts; the play is violently attacked by the critics Rebatet and Laubreaux. August 27: Cocteau completes editing *Renaud et Armide (Renaud and Armide)*, a play written for Marais, who briefly joined the Comédie Française. October 4: He writes the first of a series of articles for *Comoedia, "Le Foyer des Artistes"* ("The Home of

Artists"). At the end of October, a revival of *Les Parents terribles* is staged at the Théâtre du Gymnase. Closed by the Prefect of Police, it reopens at the end of December. Cocteau meets Paul Morihien and Jean Genet. *Allégories (Allegories)* and *Dessins en marqe des Chevaliers de la table ronde (Drawings in the Margins of Knights of the Round Table)* are published. Cocteau designs the sets and costumes for *La Main Passe (The Hand Passes)* by Feydeau.

1942   May 23: *Comoedia* publishes Cocteau's "*Salut à Breker*" ("Salute to Breker"), who was Hitler's favorite sculptor. He writes the dialogues for *Le Baron fantôme (The Phantom Baron)*, a film by Serge de Poligny in which he plays a role. He testifies in favor of Genet.

1943   January 20: Cocteau's mother dies. April 13: *Renaud et Armide* is produced at the Comédie-Francaise. June: Cocteau begins filming *L'Etérnel Retour (The Eternal Return)*, with Jean Delannoy. August 29: He is beaten up by the militia. He spends the autumn in Brittany, where he works on *Léone*. *Le Mythe du Greco (The Myth of El Greco)* is published. The Théâtre de l'Alliance Française presents a production of *L'Épouse injustement soupçonnée (The Unjustly Suspected Wife)*, which Cocteau wrote in 1922.

1944   February 28: Max Jacob, on his way to the prison camp of Drancy, writes a note to Cocteau, who tries in vain to obtain his release. July 5–6: Jean Desbordes is arrested and tortured to death by the Gestapo.

1945   August 27: Cocteau begins shooting the film of *La Belle et la bête (Beauty and the Beast)*, with Jean Marais playing the beast. He is hospitalized at the end of October with a skin ailment. *Léone* and *Portrait de Mounet-Sully (Portrait of Mounet-Sully)* are published. Cocteau's verse is included in the anthology *Poètes d'aujourd'hui (Poets of Today)* and Claude Mauriac publishes his *Jean Cocteau ou la vérite du mensonge (Jean Cocteau or the Truth of the Lie)*. Cocteau writes the dialogue for Bresson's film, *Les Dames du Bois de Boulogne (The Ladies of the Bois de Boulogne)*.

1946   The production of the ballet *Le Jeune Homme et la mort* *(The Young Man and Death)* at the Théâtre des Champs-Elysées. Cocteau spends the summer at Verrières with Louise de Vilmorin. December 20: The Théâtre Hebertot presents a production of *L'Aigle à deux têtes (The Eagle with Two Heads)* created in Brussels. The publication of Cocteau's *Oeuvres complètes (Complete Works)* by Marguerat is begun (interrupted in 1951). *La Crucifixion (The Crucifixion)* is published. *La Belle et la bête* receives the Louis-Delluc prize.

1947   Cocteau, with Marais, buys the property and house at Milly-la-Forêt (Seine-et-Oise). May: Roberto Rossellini films *La Voix humaine* with Anna Magnani. Pierre Billon films the adaptation of Cocteau's *Ruy Blas*. July: Cocteau meets Edouard Dermit (whom he is to "adopt" as his son). October: the shooting of *L'Aigle à deux têtes* begins. *La Difficulté d'être (The Difficulty of Being)* is published. *Les Enfants terribles* is adapted for radio.

1948   June: Cocteau travels to London to present the film *L'Aigle à deux têtes*. He films *Les Parents terribles*. He does the commentaries for Swoboda's film, *Noces de sable (Weddings of Sand)*, and for *La légende de Sainte Ursule (The Legend of Saint Ursula)*, the film by Emmer. He completes cartoons for the tapestry *Judith et Holopherne (Judith and Holophernes)* for Aubusson. December 13: *L'Amour et son amour (Love and His Love)*, a ballet by Babilée with sets and costumes by Cocteau, is performed at the Théâtre des Champs-Elysées. End of December: Cocteau visits New York. *Poèmes*, the first two volumes of *Théâtre* (at the *Nouvelle Revue Française)*, *Reines de la France (Queens of France)* and *Drôle de ménage (The Odd Household)* are published.

1949   January 13: Cocteau returns to Paris from America. February 1: Christian Bérard dies. March 6–May 24: Cocteau takes a theatrical tour to the Near East with Marais and Dermit. The repertory includes Racine, Cocteau, Anouilh, and Sartre. August: He organizes the first film festival for banned films at Biarritz. He begins filming *Orphée (Orpheus)*. September 3: Cocteau is decorated as a Chevalier of the Legion of Honor. October 17: A production of Tennessee Williams's *Streetcar Named Desire* (adapted by Cocteau) opens at the Théâtre Edouard VII. *Maalesh, Journal d'une tournée de théâtre (Maalesh, A Theatrical Tour of the Middle East), Lettre aux américains (Letter to the Americans),* and *Théâtre de Poche (Pocket Theatre)* are published. December: Cocteau starts to film *Les Enfants terribles.*

1950　Cocteau makes the acquaintance of Francine Weisweiller (a rich patron with whom he would spend a great deal of time). March 1: *Orphée* is screened at the Cannes Film Festival. June 14: The ballet *Phèdre* is produced at the Opéra, with music by Auric. Cocteau spends the summer at the Weisweiller villa at Saint-Jean-Cap-Ferrat, where he begins decorating its interior with murals. September: *Orphée* wins the International Film Critics Prize at the Venice Film Festival. Cocteau shoots *Coriolan (Coriolanus),* an unreleased 16mm film, with Josette Day and Jean Marais.

1951　Cocteau records for radio his *Entretiens avec André Fraigneau (Interviews with André Fraigneau)* at the end of January. April: He is made chairman of the Society of Authors and Composers. He begins to edit a personal journal, *Le Passé défini (The Past Definite).* (The first volume is published in 1983.) In the spring he travels to Italy with Francine Weisweiller and Edouard Dermit. He spends the summer at Saint-Jean-Cap-Ferrat, where he shoots the unreleased 16mm film *La Villa Santo Sospir.* December 20: the production of *Bacchus* at the Théâtre Marigny. An exchange of violent polemics between Cocteau and François Mauriac takes place in *Le Figaro littéraire* and *France-soir.* The publication of *Jean Marais* and of *Entretiens autour de cinématographe (Conversations About Film).* Cocteau contributes the commentaries for the films *Le Rossignol et l'Empereur de Chine (The Nightingale and the Emperor of China),* by Trnka, and for *Venise et ses Amants (Venice and Her Lovers)* by Emmer. *L'Eternel Retour* is adapted for radio.

1952　January 18: An exhibition of Cocteau's works opens in Munich. May 14: Stravinsky directs *Oedipus Rex* at the Théâtre des Champs-Elysées. June 12–27: Cocteau takes a cruise in the

Greek islands with Francine Weisweiller and Dermit. October 18: He attends the German production of *Bacchus* in Dusseldorf. He publishes *Le Chiffre sept (The Number Seven)*, *Gide vivant (The Living Gide)*, *Le Journal d'un inconnu (Diary of an Unknown Man)*. He writes *L'Apocalypse*, an oratorio for which Claoue composed the score a few years later.

1953   May 9: The ballet *La Dame à la licorne (The Lady and the Unicorn)* opens in Munich. Cocteau is made chairman of the jury of the Cannes Film Festival. In the summer he takes his first trip to Spain. The publication of *Appoggiatures (Appoggiaturas)* and of *Démarche d'un poète (A Poet's Gait)*. He does the commentary for the film *Rouge est mis (Red is Played)*, a film made by Barrière and Knapp.

1954   February: Cocteau visits Austria. May: He goes to Spain, where he discovers bull fighting. June 10: He suffers a heart attack in Paris. He convalesces at Saint-Jean-Cap-Ferrat. August 3: Colette dies. *Clair-obscur (Chiaroscuro)* and *Poésies 1946–1947 (Poems 1946–1947)* are published. Cocteau contributes to Seggelke's film, *Une mélodie, quatre peintres (One Melody, Four Painters)*. He does numerous paintings and posters.

1955   January 10: He succeeds Colette at the Académie royale de langue et de littérature française de Belgique. May: There is an exhibition of his paintings in Rome. October 1: He attends a reception at the Académie royale. October 20: He attends a reception at the Académie Française.

1956   February: Cocteau is in Saint Moritz in Switzerland. During the spring he begins to decorate the chapel of Saint-Pierre at Villefranche-sur-mer. June 12: He receives an honorary doctorate at Oxford University. *Poèmes 1916–1955 (Poems 1916–1955)* are published. *Le Grand Ecart* is adapted for radio. Cocteau makes lithographs and starts working in pottery.

1957   March: Cocteau is elected an honorary member of the National Academy of Arts and Letters (U.S.A.). During the summer he works on the decorations for the marriage hall at the Hôtel de Ville in Menton. October: His work is exhibited at the

Galerie Matarosso in Nice. *La Corrida du ler mai (The First of May Bullfight)* and *Entretiens sur le Musée de Dresden (Conversations on the Dresden Museum)*, which he coauthored with Aragon, are published. He does the commentary for *A l'Aube du monde (At the Dawn of the World)*, a film by Lucot. Jacques Démy films *Le Bel Indifférent*.

1958 January 13: Cocteau's sister, Martha, dies. June: Two frescoes for the exhibition *Terre et Cosmos (Earth and the Cosmos)* are installed. July: Cocteau has an exhibition of his pottery at Villefranche-sur-mer. He travels to Vienna, where Herbert von Karajan is directing *Oedipus Rex*. Cocteau takes part as a member of the chorus. He continues on to Venice, where he makes drawings as models for the glass blowers at Murano. September 19: He speaks before Queen Elizabeth in the auditorium of the Brussels World Fair. His talk is on "The Secret Weapons of France." November 14: An exhibition of his pottery opens at Lucie Weill's gallery in Paris. *Paraprosodies* is published, the film *Django Reinhardt* is presented, and Cocteau collaborates on *Musée Grévin* by Jean Masson and Jacques Démy.

1959 Cocteau falls ill at Saint-Jean-Cap-Ferrat. January 28: *La Dame à la licorne* premieres at the Opéra. February 6: A production of *La Voix humaine* opens at the Opéra-Comique. March 19: An exhibition of paintings by Edouard Dermit opens in Paris. Cocteau creates sets for an open-air theater at Cap d'Ail in May. June 12: The mime-drama *La Poète et sa muse (The Poet and His Muse)* is presented at the Spoleto Festival. June and July: Cocteau works on the decoration of the Chapel of Saint-Blaise-des-Simples at Milly-la-Fôret. September: The filming of *Le Testament d'Orphée (The Testament of Orpheus)* begins. November 4: Stravinsky conducts *Oedipus Rex* in London (with Cocteau in the chorus). During this visit to London, Cocteau decorates Notre-Dame-de-France, a London church. *Gondole des morts (Gondola of the Dead)* and *Poésie critique A (Poetry Criticism A)* are published. Cocteau contributes the preface to Peyrefitte's *l'Exilé de Capri (Banished in Capri)*.

1960 February 10: *Le Testament d'Orphée* is shown in Paris. June 27: Cocteau is elected Prince of Poets (a public dispute follows his election). August and October: He travels to Spain. October 3: Cocteau's adaptation of the play *Dear Liar* opens at the Théâtre de l'Athénée. *Nouveau Théâtre de poche (New Pocket Theater)* and *Poésie critique 2 (Poetry Criticism 2)* are published.

1961 March 1: Cocteau is promoted to Commander of the Legion of Honor. May: He vacations in Marbella, where he paints four panels. July 15: An exhibition opens of his drawings in colored pencil. August-October: He returns to Marbella. December 3: His brother Paul dies. *Cérémonial espagnol du phénix (Spanish Ceremony of the Phoenix)* and *La Partie d'échecs (The Chess Game)* are published. Cocteau collaborates on Delananoy's film *La Princesse de Clèves (The Princess of Cleves)*. *Thomas l'Imposteur* is adapted for radio.

1962 May 1: The Comédie-Française production of *L'Improptu du Palais-Royal (Improvisation at the Palais-Royal)* opens in Tokyo. June: An opening party for a panel Cocteau has painted at the Hôtel de Ville in Saint-Jean-Cap-Ferrat. An exhibition of Cocteau's work opens in Tokyo. During the summer he makes sketches for the stained glass windows of Saint-Maximin Church in Metz and does preparatory work for the "bastion" of Menton and the chapel of Notre-Dame-de-Jerusalem at Fréjus. August 25: He records a "Message for the Year 2000." He designs costumes and sets for the revival of *Pelléas and Mélisande* presented at the Metz Festival on September 22. September 29: Cocteau delivers an homage to Maeterlinck in Brussels. *Cordon ombilical (Umbilical Cord)*, *Picasso 1919–1961*, and *Requiem* are published.

1963 April 14–20: Paul Seban films Cocteau at Milly-la-Fôret for *Portraits-Souvenir*. April 22: Cocteau has a heart attack in Paris. July 5: He returns to Milly, never to leave again. With Raymond Gérôme, he writes an adaptation of *The World of Suzy Wong*. October 11: A few hours after the death of Edith Piaf, Cocteau dies.

Cocteau with his academician's sword after his election to l'Académie Française, 1955

Acknowledgments

It has been clear ever since his death in 1963 that Jean Cocteau's star continues to rise. The first true multi-media artist, Cocteau has for much of this century embodied the spirit of the French avant-garde to the American public.

To mark the twentieth anniversary of his death, the French-American Foundation has created *Cocteau Generations; Spirit of the French Avant-Garde*, a celebration of Cocteau's generative role in the arts throughout his lifetime. To further illuminate the themes and perspectives which underlie the entire celebration, the French-American Foundation also commissioned this collection of essays by American and French experts on Cocteau's place in the arts of his period.

My debts are legion to the many individuals and organizations, in France and the United States, who helped transform this celebration from dream to reality. For their confidence in the concept from the very beginning, I want to thank the board of directors of the French-American Foundation, and the National Endowment for the Humanities whose planning grant enabled us to blueprint the program. A talented project planning committee was invaluable in providing practical counsel: Doré Ashton, Tom Bishop, Schuyler Chapin, Pierre Georgel, Wilder Green, Alexis Gregory, Constance Jewett, Robert Littman, Denise Mitchell, Neal Oxenhandler, Ned Rorem, Roger Shattuck, Francis Steegmuller, and the late Margaretta Akermark. Signal contributions came from The National Endowment for the Arts, the American Embassy in Paris, the American Society of the French Legion of Honor, the city of Paris, the Dillon Fund, the Fondation Franco-Américaine, the French Ministry of External Relations, Friends of the French-American Foundation, Hill and Knowlton, The Rosenstiel Foundation, the Scaler Foundation, and the United States Information Agency. Generous corporate sponsorship was provided by Rémy Martin.

We were honored to have as distinguished patrons for the celebration: Claude Cheysson, French minister of external relations; Jacques Chirac, mayor of Paris; Evan C. Galbraith, United States ambassador to France; Jean-Marie Guehenno, cultural counselor of the French Embassy to the United States; Jack Lang, French minister delegate of culture; Daniel Terra, United States ambassador-at-large for cultural affairs; Bernard Vernier-Palliez, French ambassador to the United States. In addition, I would like to thank the participating organizations whose contributions of performances, readings, round tables and lectures enriched the celebration: Francine Kourilsky and the UBU Theater; Eve Adamson and the Jean Cocteau Repertory Theater; Dean Gideon Waldrop and the Juilliard School of Music; Jacqueline Hellerman and the Maison Française of Columbia University; David Noakes and the Maison Française of New York University; Jacqueline Chambord and the French Institute-Alliance Française; Tom Bishop and the Center for French Civilization and Culture, New York University; the departments of Drama and Music and the Humanities Research Center of the University of Texas at Austin.

Particular appreciation and thanks are due to the exhibition curator, Robert Littman, now director of the Museo Tamayo in Mexico City; Marie-Claude Dane, director of the Pavillon des Arts in Paris; Jan van der Marck, director of Miami's Center for the Fine Arts; Eric Mc-Cready, director of the Archer M. Huntington Art Gallery of the University of Texas at Austin; Robert Buck, director of the Brooklyn Museum; Fabiano Canosa, program director of the Public Theater in New York; Jacques Boutet, director of cultural affairs in the French Ministry of External Relations; Michel Boutinard-Rouelle, director of cultural affairs for the city of Paris; Edouard Dermit, Jean Cocteau's heir; Pierre Chanel, curator of the Cocteau Archives at Milly-la-Forêt and director of the Musée de Lunéville; and Anne de Margerie, our exhibition coordinator in France.

For keeping this binational cultural effort moving steadily forward I have primarily to thank the staff of the French-American Foundation: Vice President Constance Jewett, who served from the start as assistant project director and general trouble-shooter; and Denise Mitchell, manager of finance and administration who, as project comptroller, kept us on the financial track. President Sara Pais brought her much needed media and promotion expertise to the project at the critical moment; and her able assistant Berit Brihammar somehow created order out of records that threatened to run amok. All of these remarkable colleagues lifted my flagging spirit in the home stretch.

A final word of thanks to the French and American publics who viewed the exhibitions, saw the films, took part in the discussions, listened to the music, enjoyed the peformances, and read these essays. In doing so, they too have become participants in this celebration. It is my hope they will carry away fresh insights on the turbulent shifts in aesthetic and ethical perspectives forced by the French avant-garde, shifts which later deeply affected our own American culture.

Arthur King Peters
Project Director

Contributors

DORÉ ASHTON, professor of art history at Cooper Union, is the author of seventeen books, including *About Rothko, Robert Motherwell* (with Jack Flam), and *A Fable of Modern Art*. Professor Ashton is chairman of the PEN Freedom to Write Committee.

STEPHEN HARVEY is assistant curator of the department of film at the Museum of Modern Art in New York. Mr. Harvey was the co-director of Rediscovering French Film. His books include *Joan Crawford* and *Fred Astaire*. He is currently writing a critical study of the films of Vincent Minnelli.

NEAL OXENHANDLER is professor of romance languages at Dartmouth College. He is the editor of *French Review*. Professor Oxenhandler has been the editor of two anthologies, *Aspects of French Literature* and *French Literary Criticism*, and is the author of *Scandal and Parade: The Theater of Jean Cocteau* and *Max Jacob and Les Feux de Paris*.

ARTHUR KING PETERS, former chairman and president of the French-American Foundation, is the author of *Jean Cocteau and André Gide, An Abrasive Friendship*. A critic and translator, he has also taught French at Hunter College and is a Chevalier de l'Ordre des Arts et des Lettres.

NED ROREM is a composer, playwright, poet, and critic. His many books include *Critical Affairs*, *The Paris Diary*, *The New York Diary*, and *Setting The Tone*. He has been the recipient of numerous awards and honors, including the Pulitzer prize in music, a Guggenheim fellowship, and an award from the National Institute of Arts and Letters.

KENNETH E. SILVER is an assistant professor of fine art at New York University. He is a contributor to *Art in America* and *House & Garden*. Professor Silver is the author of the forthcoming *Esprit de Corps; The Great War and the Art of the Parisian Avant-Garde*.

ROGER SHATTUCK is commonwealth professor of French literature at the University of Virginia. His many books include *The Banquet Years* and *Wild Boy of Averyon*.

FRANCIS STEEGMULLER is a distinguished author, critic, and translator. He has been a contributor to *The New Yorker*, *Vogue*, *Partisan Review*, *The New York Review of Books*, and *The New York Times*. Mr. Steegmuller was the editor of *The Letters of Gustave Flaubert* (volumes I and II). He is the author of *Cocteau, A Biography*, for which he received a National Book Award in 1972.

PIERRE CHANEL, curator of the Musée Lunéville in France, is also curator of the Cocteau archives at Milly-la-Forêt and editor of the *Cahiers Cocteau* published by Gallimard. His works on Cocteau include the annotated *Le Passé défini*, *Album Cocteau*, and *Jean Cocteau, poète graphique*.

BERNARD DELVAILLE is an editor at Edition Robert Laffont and at Seghers in Paris. He has been a visiting professor of French literature at the University of North Carolina and is author of *Essay sur Valéry-Larbaud* and of *Paul Morand*.

Index

(Numbers in italic type refer to illustrations)

237

PHOTOGRAPHIC CREDITS

The photographers and the sources of the photographs other than those indicated in the captions are as follows: Collection Bibliothèque Forney, Paris: page 113; Bibliothèque-Musée de l'Opéra de Paris, Paris: page 90; Courtesy Fabiano Fenosa: pages 13, 199, 206; Courtesy Giraudon/Art Resource, Inc., New York: pages 38, 66, 212, 218; F. O. Gundlach, Stuttgart: jacket back; Musées des Deux Guerres Mondiales, Paris: page 95; Musées Nationaux, Paris: pages 49, 59, 60, 129, 131, 133, 167, 211, 217; Museum of Modern Art, New York: pages 184, 188, 189, 190, 194, 195, 197, 200, 201, 202, 203, 205; Paul Morihien, Paris: page 121; © 1984 The Paul Strand Foundation, Millerton, New York: page 8; © Juliet Man Ray: pages 14, 18, 27, 63, 65, 67, 69, 80, 136, 143, 157, 220, 221; Courtesy Kenneth Silver: page 85; Stock, Paris: pages 19, 115, 122, 171, 176; H. Roger Viollet, Paris: pages 32, 34, 37, 42, 46, 124, 138, 150, 152, 230; Raymond Voinquel, Paris: title page, pages 110–11